Let's Talk 3

Student's Book

Leo Jones

CAMBRIDGE
UNIVERSITY PRESS

PUBLISHED BY THE PRESS SYNDICATE OF THE UNIVERSITY OF CAMBRIDGE
The Pitt Building, Trumpington Street, Cambridge, United Kingdom

CAMBRIDGE UNIVERSITY PRESS
Cambridge, New York, Melbourne, Madrid, Cape Town, Singapore, São Paulo

Cambridge University Press
40 West 20th Street, New York, NY 10011–4211, USA

www.cambridge.org
Information on this title: www.cambridge.org/9780521776929

First published 2002
7th printing 2005
Printed in Hong Kong, China

Library of Congress Cataloging-in-Publication Data

Jones, Leo, 1943-
Let's talk 1 / Leo Jones.
    p.   cm.
"Student's book."
ISBN-13   978-0-521-77692-9 Student's Book
ISBN-10   0-521-77692-9 Student's Book
1. English language – Textbooks for foreign speakers.   I. Title: Let's talk one.
PE1128 .J624   2002
428.3´4–dc21   2001037375

ISBN-13   978-0-521-77692-9 Student's Book
ISBN-10   0-521-77692-9 Student's Book

Art direction, book design and layout services: Adventure House, NYC

Contents

Author's acknowledgments

Many people contributed their hard work, fresh ideas, helpful encouragement, and sound advice to the *Let's Talk* series.

Thank you to the **reviewers** for their suggestions: Bruce Ballard, Nick Brideson, Steven Brown, Marin Burch, Susan Caesar, Steve Cornwell, Alexandre Figueiredo, Ardis Flenniken, Donna Fujimoto, Aretha Cibele Galat, Sally Gearhart, Sheila Hakner, Christa Hansen, Timothy J. Hogan, Lisa Hori, Madeline Kim, Suzanne Koons, Brian Long, Declan Long, Christopher Lynch, Jackie Maguire, Marie Melenca, Paul Moore, Magali de Moraes Menti, Aphrodite Palavidis, Ane Cibele Palma, Nevitt Reagan, Christine Salica, Rogerio Sanches, Chuck Sandy, Davee Schulte, Benjamin Fenton-Smith, Aviva Smith, and Karen Woolsey.

I would also like to acknowledge the **students** and **teachers** in the following schools and institutes who piloted materials in the initial development stages: **Boston University,** Boston, Massachusetts, U.S.A.; **Center for English Studies,** New York City, New York, U.S.A.; **Centro Cultural Brasil-Estados Unidos,** Belém, Brazil; **Nagasaki Junior College of Foreign Languages,** Nagasaki, Japan; **Nanzen Junior College,** Nagoya, Japan; **Southern Illinois University,** Niigata, Japan; **University of Pittsburgh,** Pittsburgh, Pennsylvania, U.S.A.; **University of Southern California,** Los Angeles, California, U.S.A.

Thanks to the **editorial** and **production team:** Naomi Ben-Shahar, Sylvia P. Bloch, David Bohlke, Patti Brecht, Liane Carita, Ben Clark, Sarah Coleman, Karen Davy, Steve Day, Phyllis Dolgin, Deborah Goldblatt, Nada Gordon, Sandra Graham, Susan Johnson, Rich LePage, James R. Morgan, Kathy Niemczyk, Bill Paulk, Mary Sandre, Howard Siegelman, and Mary Vaughn.

Finally, a special thanks to the Cambridge University Press **staff** and **advisors:** Jim Anderson, Kanako Aoki, Carlos Barbisan, Kathleen Corley, Riitta da Costa, Elizabeth Fuzikava, Steve Golden, Gareth Knight, Nigel McQuitty, Andy Martin, Carine Mitchell, Mark O'Neil, Colin Reublinger, Dan Schulte, Ivan Sorrentino, Ian Sutherland, Koen Van Landeghem, Su-Wei Wang, and Ellen Zlotnick.

To the student

Let's Talk 3 is about communication. It is about listening to and understanding other people's ideas, and about sharing your ideas with your fellow students.

Be brave! Mistakes are an important part of learning. You will make progress, even if you sometimes make a mistake. Your partners and teacher will correct the mistakes that prevent you from communicating effectively.

There are 16 units in *Let's Talk 3*, each containing two lessons. The lessons include these activities:

Pair work and Group work   In these activities you can express your ideas and hear the ideas of other students in the class. There are many pair and group work exercises in the book so you will have plenty of speaking practice.

Listening exercises   In real life it is necessary to listen carefully in order to understand new information. Each listening exercise in *Let's Talk 3* is accompanied by tasks for you to do as you listen. There are charts to fill in, notes to take, questions to answer, and matching exercises where you choose the right picture for each recording. You can discuss your reaction to the recordings in the pair or group work activities that follow most listenings.

Communication tasks   In most units there is a communication task for you to do with a partner or group. Sometimes you will look at photos and decide on a story for the photos. At other times you will share information with a partner or partners. Related communication tasks are on different pages at the back of the book so that you can't read each other's information. The instructions in the lessons tell you which task to look at.

Self-study CD   The CD at the back of the book contains many of the recordings used in the classroom. On pages 92 to 107 there are exercises for you to do on your own using the CD. It's best to do these *after* you finish the lesson in class.

Grammar   On pages 114 to 121 there are grammar reference pages. These will help to answer any questions you have about grammar.

Let's Talk 3 will help you to enjoy using English while also increasing your vocabulary and improving your grammatical accuracy. But you've read enough for the moment – now, let's talk!

1A First impressions

Activity 1 **A Pair work** Look at these photos. Which people do you think already know each other?

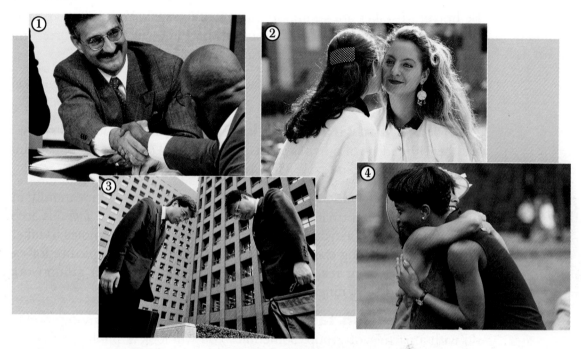

> I don't think the men in the first picture already know each other.

B Listen 🎧 You will hear the four conversations from part A. Fill in the chart. ✳

Do the people know each other well?		What do you hear that makes you think that?
1. ☐ Yes ✔ No		It's a pleasure to meet you.
2. ☐ Yes ☐ No		
3. ☐ Yes ☐ No		
4. ☐ Yes ☐ No		

C Group work Discuss these questions.
- How do you greet someone you are meeting for the first time? someone you've met once before? someone you know well?
- How do you behave if the other person is . . . ?

| a man | a child | a classmate at school | a friend's parent |
| a woman | a teacher | a colleague at work | not from your country |

> If the other person is a man, I usually shake hands.

✳ **SELF-STUDY** *see page 92*

Activity 2   **A Pair work**   Circle the words below that you don't know, and ask your partner to explain them. Use a dictionary to look up any that neither of you knows. Then add the words to the chart.

| abrupt | attentive | friendly | insincere | nosy | shy |
| aloof | calm | gracious | nervous | patient | sincere |

Positive words		Negative words	
....	....	*abrupt*	....
....	....	....	....
....	....	....	....

B Join another pair   Discuss these questions.
- Compare your charts in part A. Do any words belong in both columns?
- Which words are similar in meaning? opposite in meaning?

C Listen 🎧   You will hear three conversations. Check (✔) the person in each conversation who gives the better impression.

✔ Allen ☐ Tina   ☐ Marcus ☐ Linda   ☐ John ☐ Debbie

D Pair work   Compare your answers. Give reasons for your choices.

> *Allen gives the better impression. Tina interrupts a lot.*

Activity 3   **A Group work**   Look at these tips on how to make a good impression. Do you agree that they are important? What additional tips can you think of?

> **Introduce yourself.**   **Give and receive compliments graciously.**
> **Remember the name of the person you are talking to.**
> **Listen attentively.**   **React appropriately.**

> *It's very important to listen attentively.*   *Yes, and it's also important to ask questions.*

B Group work   Greet the people in your group, and get acquainted with everyone. Try to make a good impression.

1B Working together

Activity 1 **A Pair work** Look at these sentences about attitudes toward problem solving. Check (✔) the ones that are true for you. Then answer the questions below.

☐ I must find the answer quickly.
☐ I take as long as I need to find the answer.

☐ Working on the problem is the best part.
☐ Finding the solution is the best part.

☐ I often take the lead in solving a problem.
☐ I'm comfortable letting others work out a solution.

☐ I prefer working alone.
☐ I prefer working with others.

☐ I suggest ideas as soon as they enter my head.
☐ I think hard before I suggest ideas.

☐ I don't like to make mistakes.
☐ I don't mind making mistakes.

- Which of the attitudes above do you think are the most important for problem solving? Why?
- Are some attitudes better for some problems than for others?
- Are some people naturally better at problem solving than others?
- Are you good at solving problems? Why or why not?

> I think it's important to think before suggesting ideas. You might change your mind.

B Pair work Try to solve these puzzles.

1. What is this secret message?

23	5		8	15	16	5		25	15	21		5	14	10	15	25
W						E						E				

21	19	9	14	7		20	8	9	19		2	15	15	11
												O	O	

> What do you think it means?

> It looks like each number stands for a letter.

2. What are the next two numbers or letters in each sequence?

31 28 31 30 ___ ___   O T T F F S S ___ ___

Y Y H L Y E Y ___ ___

> Each number must represent something.

> I got the first one! There are 31 days . . .

C Listen 🎧 You will now hear the answers to the puzzles. Listen to the strategies on problem solving. Did you solve the puzzles in the same way?

A Group work Try these games.

1. Spend three minutes thinking of as many imaginative uses as you can for these everyday objects. One person should record the group's ideas in a list.

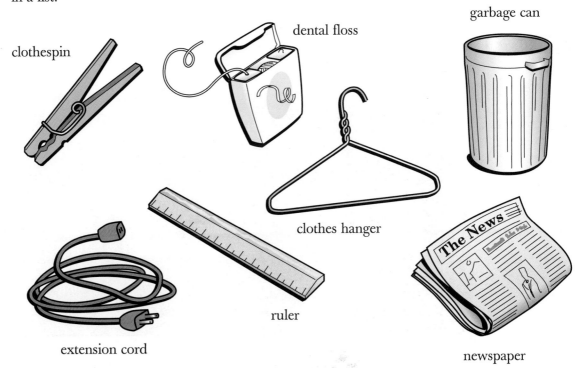

clothespin

dental floss

garbage can

clothes hanger

extension cord

ruler

newspaper

> I know. You can use dental floss to tie a package.

> And you can make a clothesline, so you can hang up wet laundry.

2. Spend two minutes using the letters in the phrase below to make as many words as you can. One person in your group should record the group's ideas in a list.

WORKING TOGETHER

> There are a lot of words: "egg," "right," "in," . . .

B Class activity Compare your lists. Then discuss these questions.
- Which group had the longest list? What was the most imaginative use for one of the objects?
- Which group had the most words? Which group came up with the longest word?
- What was the most important thing you learned about cooperative problem solving?

C Communication task Work with a partner. One of you should look at Task 1 on page 74, and the other at Task 16 on page 79. You're going to complete a puzzle together.

2A Announcements and signs

A Pair work Look at the airport departure board. Then discuss the questions below.

DEPARTURES

FLIGHT		DESTINATION	GATE	TIME	REMARK
OZ 352	ASIANA AIRLINES	SEOUL	35	08:10	DEPARTED
TG 414	THAI AIRWAYS	BANGKOK	20	08:20	LAST CALL
NH 112	ALL NIPPON AIRWAYS	OSAKA	22	08:45	BOARDING
CI 666	CHINA AIRLINES	TAIPEI	28	09:15	CHECK IN
SQ 118	SINGAPORE AIRLINES	KUALA LUMPUR	32	09:35	CHECK IN
JL 710	JAPAN AIRLINES	TOKYO	26	09:50	DELAYED
CZ 356	CHINA SOUTHERN AIRLINES	BEIJING	38	10:10	ON TIME
PR 504	PHILIPPINE AIRLINES	MANILA	23	10:25	ON TIME

- Which flight has already taken off?
- Which flight is probably leaving very soon?
- Which flight is late?

B Listen You will hear four announcements about the flights. What information has changed? Write the new information. *

Announcement 1	NH 112 – last call
Announcement 2	
Announcement 3	
Announcement 4	

C Pair work Compare your answers. Then discuss these questions.
- Which announcement was the hardest to understand? Why?
- Which was the easiest to understand? Why?
- Have you ever had difficulty understanding an important announcement? What did you do?

> Announcement . . . was the hardest to understand because I'm unfamiliar with the accent.

Activity 2 **A Pair work** Look at these real street signs from the United States – and one from Australia. What do you think they mean? Do you have any of these signs in your country?

1   2   3   4   5

6   7   8   9   10

This sign means that you can't turn left.

This one says that there's a curve ahead.

B Pair work How many did you guess correctly? Turn to page 86 to check your answers.

Activity 3 **A Work alone** Signs are effective when they use only a few words. Write your own short signs to express these meanings.

1. Please do not park here.

NO
Parking

2. If you go past this gate, a dog may attack you.

Beware
___ ___

3. Nobody except the staff can enter this room.

STAFF _____

4. Running is not allowed here.

___

Permitted

5. You need to be watchful of pedestrians.

___ Out for Pedestrians

6. Nobody should walk on the grass.

Keep ___ the grass

B Pair work Compare your answers. Then turn to page 86 to check your answers.

C Group work Design two signs of your own, and share them with the class.

2B Feelings and gestures

Activity 1 **Pair work** Look at these photos. Then discuss the questions below.

- Which words do you think describe the people in each of the photos?

annoyed	confident	furious	irritated	mad	scared
anxious	fearful	glad	joyous	proud	tense

- What has just happened in each photo?
- Would you feel the same way in each situation?

The girl in the first picture looks very proud and . . .

Activity 2 **A Pair work** Look at the pictures. What advice would you give to the people in these situations? Write your ideas on a separate piece of paper.

I would say to the boy: "You should study harder."

B Listen 🎧 Now you will hear the conversations. Fill in what was actually said.

C Pair work Act out the conversations using your own ideas or those in part B.

A Pair work Look at these gestures that people often use in the United States. Write the number of the gesture next to its meaning below.

_4_ I'm thinking.   _1_ I'm puzzled.   _3_ I love you.

_8_ You have a phone call. _9_ I'm just kidding.   _6_ Calm down.

_2_ I'm sorry.   _7_ This is a secret.   _5_ Be quiet.

B Join another pair Turn to page 86 to check your answers. Then discuss these questions.
- Which of the gestures above have the same meaning in your country?
- Which have a different meaning?
- What gestures do people in your country use to convey the ideas above?
- Are there any gestures you especially like?
- Are there any gestures you especially dislike? Why?

C Pair work Have nonverbal "conversations" using the gestures above. Can you understand what is being communicated?

3A Crime and punishment

Activity 1   **A**   **Pair work**   Look at these photos. Then discuss the questions below.

burglary

arson

forgery

littering

pickpocketing

vandalism

- What has happened or is happening in each of the photos?
- Which crimes are serious? What punishment would you give each criminal?

> *In the first photo, someone is breaking into a building.*

B   **Work alone**   Which statements do you agree with? Give each item a number from 1 to 5.

1 = strongly agree   2 = agree   3 = not sure   4 = disagree   5 = strongly disagree

1. Anyone could become a criminal under the right circumstances.	
2. Crime doesn't pay.	
3. There's too much crime on TV and in the movies.	
4. Criminals are born, not made.	
5. If wealth were distributed fairly, there would be no crime.	
6. Parents should be held responsible for crimes their children commit.	

C   **Pair work**   Compare your opinions. Do you share each other's views? Why or why not? Support your opinions with reasons.

> *I agree that anyone could become a criminal. For example, if I were . . .*

Activity 2 **A Pair work** Are these serious "crimes"? Check (✔) your opinions.

	Very serious	Somewhat serious	Not serious
1. driving over the speed limit	☐	☐	☐
2. jaywalking	☐	☐	☐
3. finding something on the street and keeping it	☐	☐	☐
4. lying about your age	☐	☐	☐
5. giving a false name	☐	☐	☐
6. not fastening your seat belt when riding in a car	☐	☐	☐
7. cheating on an exam	☐	☐	☐
8. taking something from a restaurant or hotel	☐	☐	☐
9. recording a CD onto a cassette	☐	☐	☐

B Group work Compare your answers. Which of the "crimes" are acceptable? When? Which are never acceptable?

> I think driving over the speed limit is acceptable during an emergency.

> Maybe, but it would have to be a very serious emergency.

Activity 3 **A Read/listen** 🎧 First read the news reports about crime, and try to guess the missing words. Then listen and check your answers.

① Two young thieves robbed a _camera_ store. They took photographs of each other with an _____ camera at the scene of the crime. When _____ sheets came out of the camera, they threw the _____ away. The police found the photographs later and recognized the two men.

② A couple and their _____ children woke up at 3 A.M. when they heard their _____, Mopsy, thumping its foot very loudly. They had just been burglarized. Mopsy's thumping woke them up in enough time to see a man and a woman leaving the house on _____ mountain bikes. The couple was later arrested.

③ A bank robber ordered the teller to fill a bag with cash. The teller filled it with loose cash from the other tellers. The robber left with about _____. A few minutes later, he returned with the money and _____ for what he had done. Then he _____ for the police to arrive.

④ Some burglars break into people's homes when they are on _____, but they only steal _____. What they do is _____ the homes! When the owners return to their homes, they find them freshly _____ and cleaned but with the cupboards and refrigerator empty.

B Pair work Compare your answers. Then discuss these questions.
- Which crime do you think is the most serious? the least serious?
- If you were the judge in each case, what kind of punishment would you give out?
- If you could change one law to make something legal, what would it be?

> The bank robbery was the most serious because the man . . .

3B Solving crimes

Activity 1

A Listen 🎧 You will hear part of a radio show about four famous detectives from film and fiction. Where were they from? Who created them? What were their famous cases? Listen and match by drawing lines.

Name	Nationality	Creator	Case
Sherlock Holmes	American	Agatha Christie	*The Hound of the Baskervilles*
Philip Marlowe	French	Sir Arthur Conan Doyle	*4:50 from Paddington*
Miss Marple	English	Raymond Chandler	*The Man on the Eiffel Tower*
Inspector Maigret	English	Georges Simenon	*The Big Sleep*

B Listen again 🎧 Which case sounds the most interesting? Why? ✳

C Pair work Discuss these questions.
- Are any fictional detectives popular in your country? Which ones?
- What's your favorite detective story or movie?

D Group work Look at this picture, and discuss these questions.
- Which case in part A do you think this picture is from?
- What do you think has just happened? What do you think is going to happen next?
- What is the story behind the picture? Create your own story.

✳ **SELF-STUDY** *see page 94*

Activity 2   **A Pair work** Imagine that your friend John has mysteriously disappeared. Look at his desk, and use the clues to figure out what happened to him.

> I think John got into trouble and had to leave the country.

> Yes, but he didn't go alone. There are two receipts for airline tickets.

B Communication task   Work in groups of three. One of you should look at Task 2 on page 74, one at Task 18 on page 80, and one at Task 32 on page 84. You're going to find out some more detailed information about the clues above. Share your information and make up a story.

C Group work Discuss these questions.
- If you could disappear for a week, where would you go? What would you do?
- If people looked in your bag right now to look for "clues," what would they find? What would they learn about you?
- What would people find if they visited your room? What would they learn about you?

> If I could disappear, I'd definitely go to a quiet beach.

4A That's strange!

Activity 1 **A Pair work** Look at this picture by M. C. Escher. Then discuss the questions.
- What is your first impression of this picture? What is each person doing?
- Turn the picture. What is each person doing?
- How would you explain the odd building?

B Pair work Create a short story based on the picture. These questions can guide you.
- What is the setting and time?
- Who are the people?

> It looks like a hotel. I think the people are . . .

C Listen 🎧 Michael and Karen are in a museum discussing the picture by Escher. What are they saying about the picture? Complete the chart.

	Setting	Time	People
Michael			
Karen			

14   Unit 4   Mysteries and surprises

Activity 2   **A**   **Pair work**   Look at these pictures. What makes each picture strange?

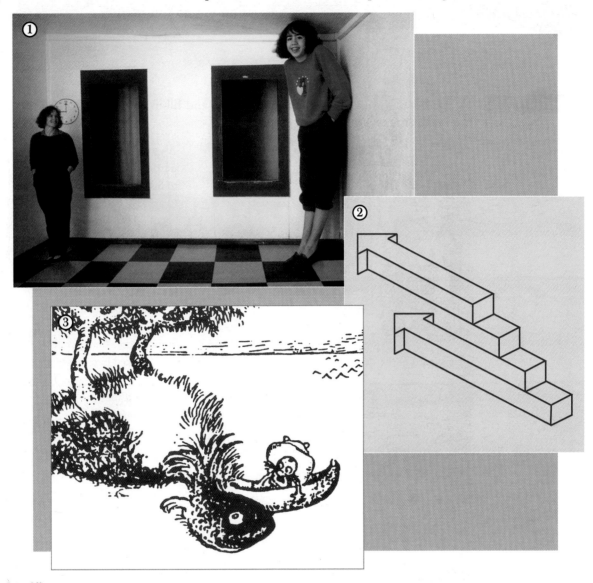

In the third picture, you get a different picture when you turn it upside down.

B   **Join another pair**   Compare your reactions to the pictures.

Activity 3   **A**   **Communication task**   👁👁   Work in groups of four. Two of you should look at Task 12 on page 77, and the other two at Task 19 on page 80. Each pair is going to have a different picture to look at and discuss.

B   **Join another pair**   Work with a different pair. Ask them about the story behind their pictures, and tell them about yours.

C   **Group work**   Discuss these questions.
- What do you like and dislike about the pictures in this lesson? the pictures in Tasks 12 and 19?
- Do you enjoy going to art museums? Why or why not?

Activity 1 **A Listen** 🎧 Listen to these two stories, and fill in the blanks. Try to predict how each story will end.

① A boy dreamed of _____ to Brazil. One day, he took his passport to the _____ and looked for a family with lots of _____ and lots of _____. He followed the family through passport control. He waited in the departure area and again _____ the family onto the _____. The cabin crew found him a _____ on the plane, and he went all the way to Rio de Janeiro. In Rio, he continued to follow the family.

ENDING: The boy lost the family when they _____.

② A young man was introducing himself to his new neighbors. Outside one _____, he saw a big dog. When he went up to ring the _____, the dog followed. He assumed it belonged to the _____ in the house. An older couple asked him in and gave him coffee and _____. The dog ate one of his cookies off the _____ and then climbed on the young man's _____. Later the young man _____ the couple and left.

ENDING: When the young man left, the woman called after him: "_____!"

> I think the boy lost the family when they went to claim their bags.

B Listen again 🎧 You will hear the stories again, this time with their endings. Check your answers. Did you guess the endings? ✳

C Pair work Read these newspaper stories from the United States. Do you think they really happened?

① While a coat was being made, a snake was accidentally sewn into the lining. When a customer later bought the coat, the snake bit him.

② A student got his college tuition completely paid for. He did it by taking out a newspaper ad asking for one cent from everyone who read the ad.

> That could have happened if the factory were in a rural area.

> Do you think so? It's possible, but it's hard to believe.

D Communication task 👓 Work with a partner. One of you should look at Task 4 on page 75, and the other at Task 20 on page 80. You're going to tell a story.

Activity 2   **A Pair work** Match these superstitions found in North America.

1. **If you carry a rabbit's foot with you,** _h_
2. **If your ears are burning,** ....
3. **If you see a penny on the ground and pick it up,** ....
4. **If you throw a coin into a fountain and make a wish,** ....
5. **If you spill salt,** ....
6. **If you say something has been good so far,** ....
7. **If a black cat crosses your path,** ....
8. **If you break a mirror,** ....

a. **you will have bad luck unless you throw some over your left shoulder.**
b. **something terrible will happen.**
c. **someone somewhere is talking about you.**
d. **you will have seven years of bad luck.**
e. **knock on wood to keep it that way.**
f. **you will have good luck for the rest of the day.**
g. **it will come true.**
h. **you will have good luck.**

B Pair work Turn to page 86 to check your answers. Then discuss these questions.
- Do you think you are a very superstitious person? Why or why not?
- Do you ever do any of the things in part A?
- What superstitions are common in your country?
- Why do you think superstitions exist?

I'm superstitious about some things. For example, I always . . .

Activity 3   **A Pair work** Look at these symbols of good luck in North America. What are some good-luck symbols in your country?

 rabbit's foot   horseshoe   four-leaf clover   shooting star

B Group work Complete this chart with information about superstitions in your own country. Share your answers with the group, and then discuss the questions below.

lucky or unlucky numbers	
lucky or unlucky days	
things to avoid doing	
animals that bring good or bad luck	
foods that bring good or bad luck	
how you make a wish	
how to turn bad luck into good luck	

- Do you have a personal lucky number? color? day? food?
- Do you have a lucky coin, ring, or other object that you always carry with you?
- What do you do if you want to be lucky? to avoid being unlucky?

Review puzzles

Puzzle A

Use the clues to complete the puzzle with words from Unit 1.

Across

1. Don't be upset if you .... a mistake.
2. Do you .... when you meet someone for the first time?
3. Someone who asks too many personal questions is .... .
4. me
5. "You look wonderful!" is a .... .
6. If you can't guess the answer, should I give you a .... ?
7. If you don't mind waiting, you're a .... person.
8. What's the solution to this .... ?
9. Can you .... this puzzle?
10. I have a very busy .... .
11. the answer to a problem or puzzle
12. The next number in the .... 1 - 4 - 9 - 16 is 25.
13. It's a .... to meet you.
14. someone in the same class as you
15. If meeting new people makes you nervous, you are .... .
16. Always try to make a good first .... .
17. Do you often take the .... in solving a problem?
18. another word for cold and unfriendly
19. What does the abbreviation USA .... ?

Down

20. If you've never met a person before, you can say, ".... .... ?"

Puzzle B

**1. Here are 6 scrambled words.
Unscramble the letters to make words
from Lesson 2A.**

teag — g <u>a</u> <u>t</u> <u>e</u>
stationedin — d _ _ _ (_) _ _ _ _ _
tarepuder — d _ _ _ _ _ _ _ _
dogbrain — b _ (_) _ _ _ _
canteenmunon — a _ _ _ (_) _ _ _ _ _
prorait — a _ (_) _ _ _ _

**2. Here are 6 more scrambled words. Unscramble
the letters to make words
from Lesson 2B.**

xosaniu — a <u>n</u> <u>x</u> <u>i</u> <u>o</u> <u>u</u> <u>s</u>
zedpulz — p _ _ _ _ _ _
riterdita — i _ _ _ _ _ (_) _ _
sente — t _ (_) _ _
surifuo — (f) _ (_) _ _ _ _
drasce — s _ _ _ _ _

3. Now use the letters in the circles above to complete the sentence.

"Have _ _ _ on your _ _ _ _!"

Puzzle C

There are 18 words from Unit 3 in this word search puzzle. How many can you find? They all have something to do with CRIME.

```
F  W  H  M  D  S  V  P  N  C  A  S  E  U  B
C  O  E  B  J  X  J  O  O  H  V  V  I  L  U
R  V  R  A  N  L  I  L  L  E  G  A  L  J  R
I  M  J  G  L  H  G  I  D  A  J  N  I  D  G
M  S  A  J  E  T  I  C  G  T  U  D  M  D  L
I  O  A  X  A  R  H  E  T  J  B  A  N  Q  A
N  T  T  B  A  Y  Y  A  I  T  U  L  C  L  R
A  G  W  I  M  V  W  T  F  B  V  I  Y  L  Y
L  B  H  B  V  N  N  A  C  H  Q  S  L  T  V
Q  C  A  R  R  E  S  T  L  O  J  M  Q  H  B
C  X  S  T  E  A  L  O  D  K  M  U  O  I  J
D  E  T  E  C  T  I  V  E  B  I  M  I  E  M
T  P  H  Y  J  P  Y  B  T  S  D  N  I  F  G
I  N  V  E  S  T  I  G  A  T  E  G  G  T  S
M  M  O  F  H  G  I  N  S  P  E  C  T  O  R
```

Puzzle D

Use the clues to solve the puzzle with words from Unit 4.

Across

3. A four-leaf .... is supposed to be lucky.
8. Carrying a rabbit's foot to bring good luck is a .... .
10. It's bad luck if a .... cat crosses your path.
12. Breaking a mirror may bring you .... luck.

Down

1. Each picture on page 15 is an optical .... .
2. Who can .... the end of the story?
4. The picture looks different if you turn it .... down.
5. Some people think the number thirteen is bad .... .
6. What is the story .... the picture?
7. Make a .... and hope it comes true!
9. another word for "strange"
10. Escher created an impossible .... .
11. to stay away from

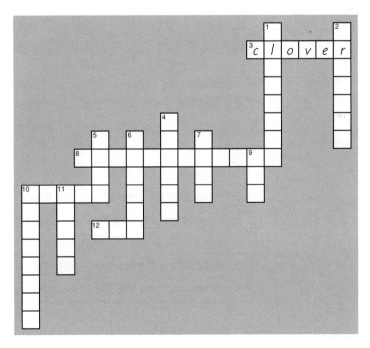

5A Happy days?

A Pair work Look at these photos. Then discuss the questions below.

- What are the students doing?
- How are these classrooms different? similar?
- Do you think you would like to be a student at any of these schools? Why or why not?

In the first picture, I think the students are completing an assignment.

B Pair work Circle the words below that you don't know, and ask your partner to explain them. Use a dictionary to look up any that neither of you knows.

after-school activities	private school	school uniform	summer school
coed school	public school	single-gender school	teacher-student ratio

C Listen Mandy, from the United States, and David, from Australia, are talking about the school system in their countries. Answer the questions.

	United States	Australia	Your country
1. Do children wear school uniforms?	No		
2. What time do classes start and finish?			
3. In what month does the school year start?			
4. Are classes single gender or coed?			
5. How long is the summer vacation?			
6. What don't you like about the school system?			

D Pair work Answer the questions about your own country. Then discuss these questions.

- How would you describe the school system in your country? Is your description more similar to Mandy's or David's?
- From what you've heard, would you recommend going to school in the U.S. or in Australia?

Activity 2 **A Pair work** Match the vocabulary with the definitions.

1. boarding school ..f..	a. a government run by the students
2. continuous assessment	b. punishment where students must stay after school
3. corporal punishment	c. grades awarded during a course, rather than after exams are taken
4. correspondence school	d. a list of students who have achieved good grades
5. detention	e. sports as part of the school curriculum
6. honor roll	f. a school that the students live at during the school year
7. physical education	g. the physical punishment of students
8. student council	h. a school that mails the student lessons, which are then mailed back for grading

B Join another pair Turn to page 86 to check your answers. Then discuss these questions.

- Does education in your country include any of the items in part A?
- Which are you in favor of? opposed to?
- If you could make one change to your school system, what would it be?

> We have physical education classes. I think that's a good thing because . . .

Activity 3 **A Listen** 🎧 Three people are talking about their first day of high school. Fill in the blanks in the summaries. ✳

Amy had attended a _____ private school. Her new public high school was huge in comparison. She didn't know what kind of _____ to wear because she had only worn a _____ before. There were ___ students in the class, and the _____ was much less strict than at her previous school. It was up to the students whether they would _____ hard or not.

Patrick _____ up too much on his first day at high school. He arrived _____ because he was new in the neighborhood. His new teacher greeted him very _____ and quickly made him feel at _____ . High school was very _____ compared with junior high school, but he enjoyed studying and joined _____ groups with other kids from his neighborhood.

Karen was _____ about being separated from her friends when she went to a new high school. But she was pleased to find her friend with her in her _____ class. She didn't find high school _____ . She got good _____ but didn't have to study hard. She enjoyed the sense of _____ in junior high school, and it was more _____ than high school.

B Group work Compare your answers. Then ask your classmates to describe their first day in:

elementary school   middle school   high school   university   this class

> What was your first day of high school like?

> Well, I remember it was very exciting. At first, I felt . . .

5B Brain power

A Pair work Look at these strategies for remembering things. Which do you use?

I make lists, write myself notes, and . . .

B Pair work Do you have a good memory? Check (✔) how good you are at remembering these things.

	Excellent	Good	So-so	Terrible
telephone numbers	☐	☐	☐	☐
passwords	☐	☐	☐	☐
personal identification numbers (PINs)	☐	☐	☐	☐
English grammar rules	☐	☐	☐	☐
faces	☐	☐	☐	☐
dates	☐	☐	☐	☐
appointments	☐	☐	☐	☐
jokes and funny stories	☐	☐	☐	☐
childhood events	☐	☐	☐	☐
directions	☐	☐	☐	☐

C Join another pair Compare your answers. Then discuss these questions.
- Do you have any tricks or techniques that help you remember things?
- What else are you good at remembering? terrible at remembering?
- Are there more similarities or more differences in your group's answers?

I'm terrible at remembering directions. I always have to draw a map.

D Pair work Who has a better short-term memory? Discuss these questions.
- What did you eat for breakfast yesterday?
- What did you wear yesterday?
- What was the last thing you said last night?
- What was the first thing you said this morning?
- Who was the last person you spoke to on the telephone?
- What was the last song you heard?
- What was the last food item you bought?
- What was the last nonfood item you bought?

I don't remember what I ate for breakfast.   *Do you remember what you wore?*

Activity 2   **A Work alone** How good are you at managing your time while studying? Circle the answers that are true for you.

Are you an effective learner?				
How often do you . . . ?	Very often	Usually	Rarely	Never
take notes during a class or lecture	3	2	1	0
rewrite notes you took	3	2	1	0
highlight passages in a text	3	2	1	0
write out study goals	3	2	1	0
take regular, short breaks while studying	3	2	1	0
get up and exercise while studying	3	2	1	0
work with a partner or study group	3	2	1	0
brainstorm ideas with a partner	3	2	1	0

B Pair work Add up the numbers from the quiz above. Turn to page 87 for an evaluation of your scores. Then discuss these questions.
- Do you agree with the evaluation? Why or why not?
- Are there any ideas in the quiz that don't seem like good ideas to you? Why?
- What other things do you think would indicate effective learning?

I don't agree with the evaluation. There are other things that can indicate effective learning, such as . . .

C Communication task Work with a partner. One of you should look at Task 5 on page 75, and the other at Task 21 on page 81. You're going to read some more learning tips.

D Group work Discuss these questions.
- What are the best ideas that you've come across in this lesson? What are the worst?
- What ideas are you likely to try?
- Do you think any of the techniques suggested for remembering things could help you become a more effective learner?

The best ideas are to take good notes, work with a partner, and . . .

6A Famous people

A Work alone Which of these qualities do you think are necessary to be successful? Check (✔) the five most important ones. Use a dictionary to look up any words that you don't know.

...... charisma	...... integrity	...... money	...... perseverance
...... discipline	...... intelligence	...... motivation	...... risk taking
...... education	...... luck	...... optimism	...... talent

B Pair work Compare your answers. Do you and your partner agree on what qualities a person needs to be successful? Defend your opinions.

C Read/listen First read the biographies of two famous people, and try to guess the missing words. Then listen and check your answers.

Jackie Chan was born in _____ in 1954. His parents were very poor, so it was difficult for them to pay the _____ bills. From the age of 7 to 17, he attended a strict _____ school for Chinese opera. His first job in movies was as a _____, but he soon got starring roles in kung-fu movies. His big breakthrough came in 1978, when he made *Snake in Eagle's Shadow*. When Jackie combined _____ with dangerous stunts, he became a big star – first in Hong Kong and then all over the _____.

Gloria Fajardo was born in _____ in 1957, and moved with her family to _____ two years later. She loved to play the guitar and sing. In 1975 she met Emilio Estefan and joined his band. Three years later, they got married. Their band, Miami Sound Machine, made several successful _____-language albums. In 1984 the band started to cross over into the _____ English-language pop market. Gloria _____ her solo career in 1989. In 1990 her tour bus was hit by a truck and Gloria was nearly _____. She fought hard to recover from her injuries, and within a _____ she was back on stage.

D Pair work Discuss these questions.
* What qualities do you think contributed to the success of each person?
* Which person would you prefer to meet? What would you ask?

> Gloria Estefan has a lot of talent, but I think her perseverance was really important.

Activity 2　**A　Pair work**　These famous people died at an early age. There is one mistake about each person. Try to find the wrong information.

Name	Minibiography
Marilyn Monroe	American actress, famous films include *Some Like It Hot* and *Breakfast at Tiffany's*
Bruce Lee	Japanese-American film star, appeared in kung-fu action films in the early 1970s
James Dean	American movie star and rock 'n' roll singer, died at the age of 24
Vincent van Gogh	Nineteenth-century German artist, famous paintings include *Sunflowers* and *Starry Night*
Princess Diana	British royal, known for her glamour and humanitarian work, died in Paris in 1999

Did Marilyn Monroe star in "Some Like It Hot"?

Yes, but she wasn't in "Breakfast at Tiffany's."

B　Pair work　Turn to page 87 to check your answers. Then discuss these questions.
- If the people in part A had lived longer, what else could they have achieved?
- Who would you like to have met? Why?

I think if Princess Diana had lived longer, she could have . . .

Activity 3　**A　Pair work**　Fill in the first two columns of the chart with the names of people who are well known in your country. Then fill in the second two columns with people who are internationally famous.

	Your country		International	
	Male	**Female**	**Male**	**Female**
TV				
Movies				
Music				
Politics				
Sports				

B　Group work　Compare your answers. Then discuss these questions.
- If a foreign visitor asked you why these people are well known in your country, what would you say about each one?
- Which people in the international columns are the most remarkable?
- What are some of their achievements? What qualities contributed to their success?
- Which people would you most like to meet? Why?

. . . is a well-known soccer player who is also in several TV commercials.

Activity 1

A Pair work Look at these sayings about money. Then discuss the questions below.

Money isn't everything.	Money doesn't grow on trees.
Money is power.	Lend your money and lose a friend.
The best things in life are free.	A fool and his money are soon parted.
Money is the root of all evil.	Money can't buy happiness.

- What do the sayings mean? In what situations would you use each of them?
- Are there any you disagree with?
- Do you have similar sayings in your culture?

"Money isn't everything" means there are many things more important than money.

B Pair work Look at these photos. What do you know about these people? You will learn about them below.

the Sultan of Brunei   Jean Paul Getty   Martha Stewart   Bill Gates

C Listen You will hear descriptions of two of the people in the photos. Complete the chart. ✳

	the Sultan of Brunei	Bill Gates
job titles	Sultan and Prime Minister	
source of wealth		
number of children		
cost of home		
number of rooms		
favorite sports		
hobbies		

D Communication task Work with a partner. One of you should look at Task 6 on page 75, and the other at Task 22 on page 81. You're going to find out about Martha Stewart and Jean Paul Getty.

Activity 2 **A Pair work** Look at these pictures. What would you say to the people in these situations? Write your ideas on a separate piece of paper.

B Listen 🎧 Now you will hear the conversations. Fill in what was actually said.

C Pair work Act out the conversations using your own ideas or those in part B.

Activity 3 **A Work alone** What would you do if you won the lottery? Make a list of what you would do first, second, third, and so on. Choose from the list below, or suggest ideas of your own.

buy a house	go on a vacation overseas	make a donation to charity
buy a yacht	give up my studies/job	buy presents for my friends and family
buy a car	put the money in the bank	learn how to do something exciting

> *If I won the lottery, the first thing I'd do is buy presents for my family.*

B Pair work Compare your lists and discuss these questions.
- What do the lists tell you about each other's attitude toward money?
- Would you like to be as wealthy as the people you've heard about in this lesson?
- Can money buy happiness? Why or why not?

> *I think you're cautious because you'd put the money in the bank.*

> *Yes, but I'd also give up my job and travel.*

7A People and languages

Activity 1 **A Pair work** Look at these photos. Then discuss the questions below.

- Where do you think these people come from? What clues are there in the photos?
- What do you think their first language is?
- Do you think any of them speak a second language? What might it be?

> The building in the third picture looks European.

> Yes, and look at the flags. Maybe they're from . . .

B Pair work Can you guess the languages for the sentences below? Try to match the sentences to the languages on the right.

1. Excuse me, could you take a photo of us, please? _c_	a. Russian
2. Kor thoat khrab, chuay thay roop hai rao noi khrab?	b. Portuguese
3. Prostite, vy ne mogli by nas sfotografirovat?	c. English
4. Disculpe, ¿puede sacarnos una foto, por favor?	d. Arabic
5. Entschuldigen Sie, können Sie bitte ein Foto von uns machen?	e. Spanish
6. Sumimasen ga, watashitachi no shashin o totte itadakemasu ka?	f. Mandarin
7. Bù hǎo yì si, qǐng nǐ tì wǒ mén paī zhào hǎo mả?	g. Korean
8. Por favor, você poderia tirar uma foto nossa?	h. Thai
9. Men fadlek, momken takhod sora lena?	i. German
10. Jesong hajiman jeohideul sajinjom jik eo jooshi kesso yo?	j. Japanese

> This one looks like it might be . . .

C Join another pair Turn to page 87 to check your answers. You will also see how to say "thank you" in each language. Then discuss these questions.
- Which language is the most familiar to you? the least familiar?
- Which language would you most like to learn? Which would be the hardest to learn?
- Would it be difficult for a visitor to your country to learn your language? Why or why not?

Activity 2 **A Listen** Can you tell the difference between an American accent and a British accent? Four people are discussing the topics they like to talk about with their friends. Check (✔) the accent you think you hear.

	Speaker 1	Speaker 2	Speaker 3	Speaker 4
American	☐	☐	☐	☐
British	☐	☐	☐	☐

B Pair work Compare your answers. Which accent are you more familiar with?

Activity 3 **A Pair work** Take this quiz together.

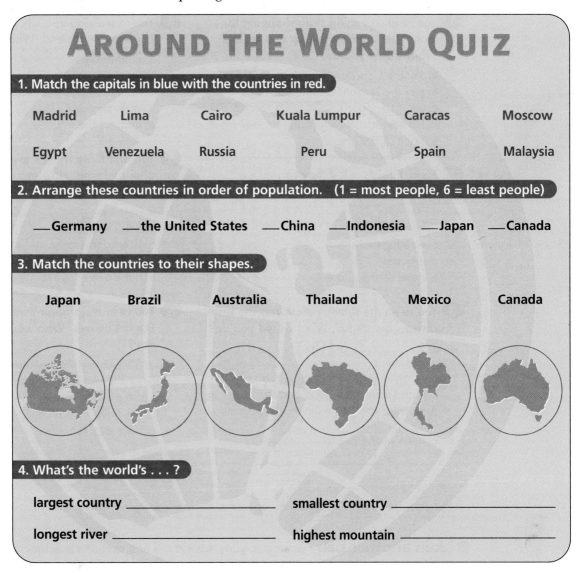

AROUND THE WORLD QUIZ

1. Match the capitals in blue with the countries in red.

Madrid	Lima	Cairo	Kuala Lumpur	Caracas	Moscow
Egypt	Venezuela	Russia	Peru	Spain	Malaysia

2. Arrange these countries in order of population. (1 = most people, 6 = least people)

—Germany —the United States —China —Indonesia —Japan —Canada

3. Match the countries to their shapes.

Japan   Brazil   Australia   Thailand   Mexico   Canada

4. What's the world's . . . ?

largest country _____   smallest country _____

longest river _____   highest mountain _____

B Join another pair Compare your answers. Then turn to page 87 to check your answers.

C Work alone Write a quiz using facts about your country. Write at least five questions.

D Group work Ask your group members your questions. Who got the most correct?

7B When in Rome ...

Activity 1 **A Pair work** Read this questionnaire with a partner, and imagine you are in each situation. Discuss your answers. Give reasons for your choices.

What would you do in your country?

1 You're in a clothing store shopping for jeans. The price on the tag is a bit high. What would you do?
   a. ask for a discount if you pay cash
   b. pay the amount on the price tag
   c. ask if the price on the tag is correct
   d. bargain for a lower price
   e. none of the above

2 Some tourists ask if they can take a photo of you. How would you feel?
   a. flattered
   b. annoyed
   c. embarrassed
   d. amused
   e. none of the above

3 You're on the subway platform. The train arrives, but it's full. What would you do?
   a. wait patiently until it's your turn to get on
   b. let the people behind you push you in
   c. push to make sure you get on
   d. wait for the next train, hoping it will be less full
   e. none of the above

4 You're walking in a city park with your boyfriend/girlfriend. What would you do?
   a. hold hands
   b. walk arm in arm
   c. walk close but not touching
   d. walk far apart
   e. none of the above

5 You and three friends take a taxi home after midnight. How much would you give the driver as a tip?
   a. nothing
   b. small change
   c. 10% of the fare
   d. 15% of the fare
   e. none of the above

6 You're in a restaurant with two friends. The bill arrives. Who would normally pay?
   a. the person who invited the others
   b. each person would pay only his/her share
   c. the person with the most money
   d. the bill would be divided equally
   e. none of the above

It would be embarrassing to bargain in a clothing store.

Why? Would it depend on the size of the clothing store?

B Join another pair Compare your answers. Then discuss these questions.
- What would most people in your country do in these situations?
- Have you ever been in similar situations? What happened?
- Think of a foreign country you've been to or would like to visit. Would your answers be different if you were in that country?

Most people would just pay the amount on the price tag.

Activity 2 **A Listen** 🎧 Norman, Lucinda, and Sung-Jae are talking about their first trip abroad. Fill in the chart. ✳

	Nationality	Place visited	Most surprising things
Norman	*Canadian*		
Lucinda			
Sung-Jae			

B Pair work Compare your answers. Then discuss these questions.
- What surprised you about what the people said?
- Which of the things that surprised them would not have surprised you?
- If you have visited another country, what things surprised you about daily life there?

Activity 3 **A Pair work** Imagine that someone from abroad will be visiting your country. What things might be different or unusual? Write down advice that would be helpful to a first-time visitor.

Situation	Advice
meeting someone for the first time	
greeting a friend	
starting a conversation with a stranger	
going to someone's house for dinner	
eating in a restaurant	
shopping	
sight-seeing and traveling	

B Join another pair Share your information. Are there any similarities in your lists?

C Group work Imagine that a visitor to your country doesn't follow your advice. What would happen?

> *You shouldn't tip in a restaurant. If you do . . .*

Activity 1　**A** **Pair work** Look at these inventions. What do you think they are used for? How do they work?

B **Listen** 🎧 You will hear descriptions of the inventions. Write down the invention, and take notes on how it works. Were your predictions correct?

Invention	How it works
1.	
2.	

C **Pair work** Look at these words that are used to describe products and inventions. Which ones would you use to describe the inventions above?

affordable	easy to use	expensive	inefficient	unattractive	useful
attractive	efficient	impractical	practical	unwieldy	worthless

> *The first invention looks practical and easy to use.*

D **Group work** Discuss these questions.
- If you had to buy one of the inventions above, which would you choose? Why?
- Which invention do you think would sell better? Why?
- What factors are important to you when you buy something? Make a group list.

E **Group work** Brainstorm with your group some common everyday annoyances or problems you face. Invent something to solve one of the problems, and describe how it would work.

> *I don't like it when my glasses get wet when it rains.*

A **Listen** 🎧 You will hear instructions involving paper, a pencil, and a paper clip. Make sure you have the necessary items, and then follow the instructions.

B **Group work** What else can you make from paper? Explain to your group members how to make something with the remaining small pieces of paper.

> *Take a piece of paper, and fold it in half like this. Then fold it in half again.*

C **Communication task** 👥 Work with a partner. One of you should look at Task 7 on page 76, and the other at Task 23 on page 81. You will each have a drawing to explain to your partner. Use the box below as your sketch pad.

1	2	3	4	5	6	7	8	9	10
11	12	13	14	15	16	17	18	19	20
21	22	23	24	A	B	C	D	E	F
G	H	I	J	K	L	M	N	O	P
Q	R	S	T	U	V	W	X	Y	Z

D **Communication task** 👥 Work in groups of four. Two of you should look at Task 8 on page 76, and the other two at Task 24 on page 82. You're going to practice explaining how to do something.

A **Work alone** Complete these sentences with your own ideas.

> The most useful thing ever invented was the _____.

> One modern convenience I can't do without is _____.

> It was easy for me to learn how to use a _____.

> It was difficult for me to learn how to use a _____.

> I wish someone would invent a _____.

> One modern convenience I can do without is _____.

> I wish someone could explain to me how a _____ works.

B **Pair work** Compare your answers. Give reasons.

> *The most useful thing ever invented was the telephone. I would be so lonely without it!*

8B User-friendly?

Activity 1

A Pair work Look at these inventions. Then discuss the questions below.

electronic organizer

navigation system

cell phone

DVD Walkman

wristwatch alarm

digital camera

- Which of these inventions do you use? How do they work?
- Do any of the inventions have any disadvantages?
- What did people do before they had these inventions?

B Listen 🎧 You will hear five people talking about frustrations they've had with technology. What item or product are they discussing? What was their problem? ✳

	Item/Product	Frustration
Daniel	remote controls	
Rosa		
Bob		
Susan		
Frederick		

C Group work Ask the members of your group to name two products they have recently acquired. Then discuss these questions about each.
- What does it do? Why did you get it?
- How has it changed your daily life? Would you recommend it to a friend?
- Is there anything you don't like about it?

✳ **SELF-STUDY** *see page 99*

A Work alone Check (✔) the three items below that are the most difficult to operate. Then compare with a partner, and answer the questions together.

☐ ATM	☐ computer	☐ pager
☐ car radio	☐ fax machine	☐ VCR
☐ cell phone	☐ microwave oven	☐ wristwatch alarm

- Did you agree on any of the items? Which ones?
- What makes the items difficult?
- What other familiar inventions are difficult to operate?

B Listen 🎧 You will hear people giving instructions on how to operate different things. Guess what is being described.

1	
2	
3	

It might be a computer.   *No, I don't think so. It sounds like . . .*

C Group work Think of another gadget you know how to operate. Without saying what it is, explain how to operate it. Who can guess what it is?

This is something found in many kitchens.
To operate it, you first plug it in. Then you . . .

D Pair work How easily can you do these things? Rate your abilities using the numbers below. Add up the numbers, and then look on page 88 for an interpretation of your score. Do you agree with the results?

4 = impossible   3 = very difficult   2 = difficult   1= fairly easy   0 = no problem

How multiskilled are you?

Can you . . . ?

○ speak a foreign language	○ stop a watch from beeping on the hour
○ surf the Internet	○ program a car radio to a new station
○ send e-mail messages	○ type on a keyboard using all your fingers
○ drive a car	○ thread a needle and sew on a button
○ cook a meal for four people	○ program a VCR
○ fix a flat tire on a bike	○ put up some shelves
○ replace a camera battery	○ heat up milk in a microwave oven
○ operate a washing machine	○ fix a leaky faucet

E Join another pair Brainstorm some ways to learn how to do the things in part D.

You can look in the user's manual.   *Yes, or you could ask a friend to help you.*

Review puzzles

Puzzle A

Use the clues to complete the puzzle with words from Unit 5.

Across

1. Most students look forward to .... vacation.
2. .... education includes sports and exercise.
3. A student in a private school wears this.
4. Drama and sports are often ....-.... activities.
5. In a study group you can .... ideas.
6. .... punishment is illegal in most countries.
7. Staying after school as punishment is called .... .
8. .... the words you want to remember.
9. With .... assessment, grades are awarded during the course.
10. .... is important; otherwise, no one can study.
11. Work with a .... .
12. The public school .... is controlled by the government or state.
13. Students live in dormitories in a .... school.
14. Most people find it harder to remember .... than names.
15. Everyone has to study hard if a school is .... .
16. I use a notebook to help me remember .... .
17. Some people find it hard to remember .... .
18. Before you can read your e-mail, you have to type in your .... .

Down

19. When you study it's efficient to take .... , ...

Crossword grid:
19. / 1. s u m m e r
2.
3.
4. -
5.
6.
7.
8.
9.
10.
11.
12.
13.
14.
15.
16.
17.
18.

Puzzle B

1. Here are 6 scrambled words. Unscramble the letters to make words from Lesson 6A.

crashaim	c h a (r) i s m a
tiny tiger	i _ _ _(_)_ _ _ _
vitamintoo	m _ _ _ _ _ _ _ _ _
tunerof	f (_) _ _ _ _ _
moistimp	o _(_)_ _ _ _ _
letant	t _ _ _ _ _

2. Here are 6 more scrambled words. Unscramble the letters to make words from Lesson 6B.

chri	(r) i c h
shapespin	h _ _ _ _ _ _ _(_)_
torylet	l _ _ (_)_ (_)_ _
sevenexpi	e _ _ (_)_ _ _ _ _
wepro	p _(_)_ _
whylate	w _ _ _ _ _ _

3. Now use the letters in the circles above to complete the sentence.

"Money doesn't _ _ _ _ on _ _ _ _ _!"

Puzzle C

There are 20 words from Unit 7 in this word search puzzle. How many can you find? They all have something to do with COUNTRIES, LANGUAGES, or CONTINENTS.

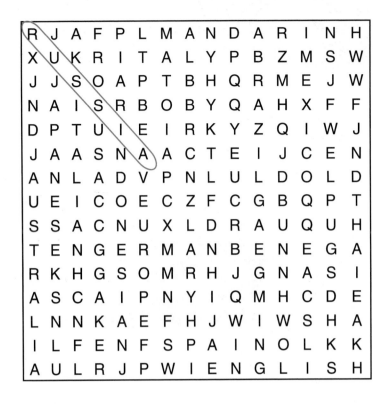

```
R  J  A  F  P  L  M  A  N  D  A  R  I  N  H
X  U  K  R  I  T  A  L  Y  P  B  Z  M  S  W
J  J  S  O  A  P  T  B  H  Q  R  M  E  J  W
N  A  I  S  R  B  O  B  Y  Q  A  H  X  F  F
D  P  T  U  I  E  I  R  K  Y  Z  Q  I  W  J
J  A  A  S  N  A  A  C  T  E  I  J  C  E  N
A  N  L  A  D  V  P  N  L  U  L  D  O  L  D
U  E  I  C  O  E  C  Z  F  C  G  B  Q  P  T
S  S  A  C  N  U  X  L  D  R  A  U  Q  U  H
T  E  N  G  E  R  M  A  N  B  E  N  E  G  A
R  K  H  G  S  O  M  R  H  J  G  N  A  S  I
A  S  C  A  I  P  N  Y  I  Q  M  H  C  D  E
L  N  N  K  A  E  F  H  J  W  I  W  S  H  A
I  L  F  E  N  F  S  P  A  I  N  O  L  K  K
A  U  L  R  J  P  W  I  E  N  G  L  I  S  H
```

Puzzle D

Use the clues to solve the puzzle with words from Unit 8.

Across

1. Water comes out of this.
5. Which .... advances simplify everyday life?
6. You used a .... clip in Lesson 8A.
8. An invention which isn't useful is .... .
11. A handheld electronic device needs this.
13. You send and receive e-mail on this.
15. the opposite of 8 across

Down

1. Which .... is more important when buying something: price or design?
2. having no value at all
3. You can heat food up in a .... oven.
4. You can listen to the news on the .... .
5. It's hard to use 13 across if you can't .... .
7. Use this to tell someone you want them to call you.
9. It's an .... when you can't find your remote control.
10. an electronic noise
12. You can use a .... camera with 13 across.
14. of use

9A Staying healthy

A Pair work Here are some different ways people exercise. Look at the pictures, and discuss the questions.

Tae-Bo

water aerobics

indoor rock climbing

- Which of these words would you use to describe the activities?

| difficult | entertaining | fun | relaxing | tedious |
| effective | exhausting | inexpensive | strenuous | worthwhile |

> Tae-Bo looks strenuous, but fun.

- Which of the activities are you familiar with?
- Which have you tried? Which would you like to try? Why?

B Group work Look at these different treatments people use to stay healthy. Turn to page 88 to find out about each treatment. Then discuss the questions.

acupuncture

aromatherapy

chiropractic adjustment

massage

herbal medicine

reflexology

- Have you tried any of these treatments?
- Which treatment(s) would you like to try?

> I've tried massage. It's very relaxing.

Activity 2 **A Pair work** What advice would you give someone on how to lead a healthier life? Number these ideas in order of importance (1 = most important, 8 = least important).

☐ Take vitamin supplements.   ☐ Avoid eating red meat.
☐ Avoid stress.   ☐ Sleep eight hours a night.
☐ Do something fun every day.   ☐ Walk as often as possible.
☐ Eat plenty of fruits and   ☐ Spend time with friends
  vegetables.   and family.

It's really important to avoid stress. People who are relaxed live longer.

B Listen Joseph, Amanda, and Brad are telling their friend Mary how they feel. Write down each person's problem in the chart below.

C Pair work Now write down the advice you would give to each person.

D Listen You will now hear Mary responding with her advice. Write it down. Is Mary's advice similar to yours? Do you agree with it?

	Problem	Your advice	Mary's advice
Joseph	bad back		
Amanda			
Brad			

Activity 3 **A Pair work** It's possible to exercise while sitting down. Look at these exercises from British Airways.

Exercises for the neck and shoulders

① Slowly lean your head to one side. Rest it gently in this position for three seconds as you breathe out. ② Repeat on the other side. Do the exercise on each side three times. ③ Repeat, bending your head forward and back three times. Don't bounce, rotate, or swivel your head.

B Pair work Now help each other do the exercises. If you don't want to exercise yourself, give your partner instructions.

C Communication task Work with a partner. One of you should look at Task 11 on page 77, and the other at Task 27 on page 83. You're going to explain some more exercises to your partner.

9B Coping with stress?

Activity 1 **A Pair work** Look at these photos. Then discuss the questions below.

- Which would be the most stressful situation for you? Why?
- Which situation do you experience most often? How do you handle it?
- How would you handle the other situations?
- Are you generally active or passive in dealing with stressful situations?

> The traffic jam would be the most stressful because I'm very impatient.

B Pair work What do you think causes the highest degree of stress for the average person? Rank your answers from 1 (most stressful) to 8 (least stressful). Then turn to page 88 to check your answers. Were you surprised by the results?

...... **having trouble with your boss**	...... **starting or finishing school**
...... **having an illness or injury**	...... **going on vacation**
...... **being fired from work**	...... **having trouble with in-laws**
...... **getting married**	...... **retiring from work**

Activity 2 **A Listen** 🎧 Five people are talking about stressful situations they've had in their lives. Complete the chart. ✳

	Reason for stress	Solution
Jared	*hard to make friends at college*	
Maria		
John		
Emi		
Doug		

✳ **SELF-STUDY** *see page 100*

B Pair work Do you have stressful lives? Interview your partner.

How stressed are you?

	Yes	No
Do you find it hard to make a decision?	☐	☐
Do you have difficulty relaxing?	☐	☐
Do you feel guilty when you're relaxing?	☐	☐
Do you find it difficult to concentrate?	☐	☐
Do you often get annoyed or lose your temper?	☐	☐
Do you have difficulty falling asleep?	☐	☐
Do you often wake up during the night?	☐	☐
Do you spend too much time working or studying?	☐	☐
Do you eat too quickly?	☐	☐
Do you worry about grades?	☐	☐

C Join another pair Compare your answers. Who is under the most stress? the least stress?

D Class activity Discuss these questions.
- What causes stress in your class?
- What can you do as a class to reduce stress?

> One thing our class can do is take longer breaks.

> And something else we could try is . . .

Activity 3 **A Group work** Look at these suggestions for reducing stress. Then discuss the questions below.

Go jogging, bicycling, or swimming daily.

Stretch at regular intervals throughout the day.

Don't take on more than you can handle. Plan ahead.

Listen carefully to what others have to say.

Breathe deeply when you feel yourself getting upset.

Don't read or watch TV during meals. Eat slowly.

Take a yoga class, or learn relaxation techniques.

- Which suggestion do you think would be the most effective? the least effective?
- Which stress-reducing techniques have you tried? Which would you like to try?

B Communication task Work with a partner. One of you should look at Task 10 on page 77, and the other at Task 26 on page 82. You're going to read some additional pieces of advice for reducing stress.

Activity 1 **A Pair work** Look at these photos. Then discuss the questions below.

thunderstorm

blizzard

typhoon

flood

tornado

drought

- Which of these events occur where you live? Which have you never experienced?
- Which one is most frightening? Which does the most damage?

B Listen Tom and Anna are describing their narrow escapes from storms. What happened? Correct the mistakes in the summaries.

Tom's story: The weather was nice when Tom and his ~~girlfriend~~ *wife*, Cindy, rented a boat to go to an island for the day. When the weather got worse, they tried to head back to the island – but the boat's engine wouldn't start. The wind was getting stronger, and the boat was being driven toward the open ocean. They were rescued by two local fishermen in a tiny inflatable boat. The boat rental guy had been worried, so he used his radio to call his fishermen friends to ask them to look for Tom and Cindy. Unfortunately, he didn't know which island the couple had gone to. Luckily, the fishermen came past the right island.

Anna's story: The weather was cloudy when Anna and her friends started to walk from the valley to the top of a mountain. They were halfway up when they realized there was going to be a thunderstorm. They got very wet, but they weren't frightened. Then one of them noticed a sign pointing to a path leading to a different mountain. It was totally the wrong direction for them, but they had to escape the storm. They eventually came to a road that led to a mountain lodge, where they spent the night. They called their hotel to tell them they were in danger.

Activity 2 **A Pair work** These words are used to describe weather. Add them to the chart below under the appropriate column.

| blustery | chilly | freezing | muggy |
| breezy | drizzly | misty | sweltering |

Windy weather	Cold weather	Wet weather	Hot weather
....	....	....	....
....	....	....	....

B Join another pair Compare your answers. Can some words go under more than one column?

Activity 3 **A Pair work** Talking about the weather is a good way to "break the ice" when you meet someone new. Look at the pictures. What would you say to these people? Write your ideas on a separate piece of paper.

① Beautiful weather, isn't it?

② Do you think this sunshine will last?

③ That's for sure!

④ Oh, look at that. We're in trouble!

B Listen 🎧 Now you will hear the conversations. Fill in what was actually said.

C Pair work Act out the conversations using your own ideas or those in part B.

D Group work Think of a specific day in the past week, and describe the weather in detail. Can your classmates guess which day you are describing?

It was chilly in the morning, but later that day it became warm and sunny.

Was it the day before yesterday?

10B The ring of fire

Activity 1 **A Pair work** Look at these photos. What is happening? Describe each photo using the words in the box or your own words.

awe inspiring
destructive
devastating
frightening
magnificent
relaxing
remarkable
soothing
therapeutic
threatening
wonderful

> The scene in the first photo is devastating and destructive, but beautiful.

B Join another pair Compare your ideas. Then discuss these questions.
- Have you ever visited an active volcano or hot springs? If so, what was it like?
- What are some famous volcanoes or hot springs that you know?

> I visited some hot springs once. Soaking in the water was very relaxing and soothing.

Activity 2 **A Pair work** These words are often used when discussing volcanoes. Circle the words below that you don't know, and ask your partner to explain them. Use a dictionary to look up any that neither of you knows.

active	crater	dormant	extinct	lava
ash	crust	eruption	geyser	magma

B Listen 🎧 You will hear a lecture about volcanoes. Listen and check (✔) the true statements. ✳

1. ☐ Volcanoes are a natural way that planets cool off.
2. ☐ Eruptions occur when magma breaks through a planet's crust.
3. ☐ Extinct volcanoes are those that will probably erupt again.
4. ☐ There are very few dormant volcanoes in the world.
5. ☐ Mount Pinatubo was the largest eruption of the twentieth century.
6. ☐ Water heated by volcanic activity can be used to generate electricity.
7. ☐ The soil around Mount Vesuvius is of poor quality.
8. ☐ Old Faithful is an example of an active volcano.

Activity 3   **A Pair work** Take this quiz with a partner. Circle your answers.

WHAT DO YOU KNOW ABOUT VOLCANOES?

① **Which country has the largest number of active volcanoes?**
   a. Indonesia   b. Japan   c. Russia   d. the U.S.   e. Chile

② **Which of these countries do not have volcanoes?**
   a. Australia   b. Brazil   c. Britain   d. India   e. South Korea

③ **Which of these countries have active volcanoes?**
   a. Italy   b. New Zealand   c. Mexico   d. Peru   e. the Philippines

④ **Where is the largest volcano in the world?**
   a. Japan   b. Indonesia   c. Hawaii   d. Canada   e. Africa

⑤ **Where is the largest volcano in the solar system?**
   a. Earth   b. Venus   c. Mars   d. Jupiter   e. the Earth's moon

I think the country with the largest number of active volcanoes is . . .

B Join another pair Compare your answers.

C Group work Look at page 88 to check your answers.
Then discuss these questions.
- Which answers did you find most surprising? Why?
- What other facts do you know about volcanoes?

D Group work Imagine that a volcano is going to erupt near your town and you must evacuate immediately. You can take only three things with you. What would they be?

I'd take some extra clothing, my photograph albums, and my diary.

Why would you take your diary?

Activity 1   **A** **Pair work**   Look at these photos. What is happening in each photo? Which of the stories that would accompany these photos would you be most interested in reading?

The first story would be the most interesting because I like stories about . . .

B **Pair work**   Look at these newspaper headlines. What story do you think follows each one? Compare your ideas.

> **"Titanic" fan travels the world to break all records**

> **Robber's ID Badge Leads to Arrest**

C **Pair work**   Look at page 89, and read the stories. Which story did you find more interesting? Why?

D **Group work**   Complete these headlines. Then make up a story for each one. Compare your stories.

> **Thief Robs Restaurant Armed with** _____

> **"** _____ **Took Our Dog," Says Couple**

> **Research shows** _____ **key to successful marriage**

> **Widow leaves** _____ **to animal charity**

A thief went into a restaurant to rob it, but he didn't have a weapon. Instead, he had a . . .

Activity 2 **A Listen** 🎧 You will hear the beginning of today's news. Match each story to the correct picture. Number the pictures from 1 to 3.

B Listen 🎧 You will now hear the full news stories. Complete the summaries.

① An orangutan stopped the traffic outside _____ . It took a keeper from the zoo _____ minutes to get downtown because of the traffic. The animal showed no interest in _____ but responded when the keeper _____ to it. It held the keeper's _____ as they got into the car.

② A new method for teaching singing has been developed. Most singers are unaware of how they _____ . By wearing a _____ over your head while you sing, you can hear your voice the way _____ hear you. This can help you _____ your singing.

③ This year there are _____ contestants in the Sunset Beach sandcastle _____ – aged from 8 to _____ . The two favorites are Greg Wallace (who has won three times before), with his _____ castle, and newcomer David Bradley, with his *Star Wars* _____

C Pair work How do you think the stories end? Note down your guess.

> I think after the zookeeper got the orangutan into the car, they drove . . .

D Listen 🎧 You will hear the next day's news. Did you guess correctly?

E Communication task 👥 Work in groups of three. One of you should look at Task 9 on page 76, one at Task 25 on page 82, and one at Task 34 on page 85. You're each going to have a news story to tell each other about.

11B People and the news

A Pair work Match these people with the definitions. Then turn to page 89 to check your answers.

1. gossip columnist _d_
2. commentator _g_
3. publisher _b_
4. cub reporter _c_
5. correspondent ___
6. meteorologist ___
7. critic ___
8. anchor ___
9. editor ___
10. paparazzi ___

a. a journalist who reports on the news from a distant place
b. a person who publishes a newspaper or magazine
c. a young reporter
d. a journalist who reports on the lives of celebrities
e. the principal journalist on a TV news program
f. a journalist who reports on the weather
g. a person on TV who comments on the news
h. photographers who follow celebrities in order to take pictures of them
i. a person who prepares material for publication or presentation
j. a person who reviews movies, plays, books, and art exhibits

B Pair work Discuss these questions.
- Which job would you find the most interesting? Why?
- How often do you watch the news on TV?
- How often do you read the newspaper?

> *Being a critic would be interesting because I like to keep up with cultural events.*

C Listen 🎧 Two people are discussing the newspaper articles. Fill in the missing words.

The King of Masks

In the 1930s, an old Chinese performer teaches a _____ girl about the art of "face changing" – an ancient form of _____ storytelling using masks. Far from being the old man's salvation, however, the _____ sets in motion a _____ chain of events, which bring her newfound skills into play. Bottom line: A film festival _____.

Active hurricane season forecast

Hurricane _____ Bill Gray and his team are standing by earlier _____ of an active hurricane similar to last year's, with 14 tropical storms and 9 _____ expected. The team believes there is a 75% higher probability that a storm will come ashore in the Caribbean or along Mexico's east coast.

D Communication task 👥 Work with a partner. One of you should look at Task 3 on page 74, and the other at Task 28 on page 83. You'll be role-playing interviews with some people in the news.

Activity 2 **A** **Listen** 🎧 A reporter is interviewing Alan, Betty, and Crystal, who all witnessed the same event but disagree on some of the details. Write the name of the speaker who describes each event shown. ✳

Alan

B **Pair work** Compare your answers. Then discuss these questions.
- Which person's story is the most believable? the least believable?
- What do you think really happened?
- How would you explain the differences in their versions of the story?

Activity 3 **A** **Pair work** How do you react to the news? Read each headline and give your reaction.

Hundreds Made Homeless After Flood

Dollar at all-time high

TEACHERS TO GET PAY RAISE

Man Wins Lottery, Loses Ticket Next Day

Dog rescues two children from river

Two children rescue dog from river

> I find the one about the man losing the lottery ticket amusing because . . .

B **Group work** Think of three more headlines, and write them down. Then share your headlines, and discuss these questions.
- How did you react to these headlines?
- Which story would you like to find out more about?

Activity 1 **A Pair work** What do you think the people are talking about? Which group would you like to join?

They might be talking about business in the first picture.

But they look like they are relaxing. Maybe they're discussing . . .

B Work alone What qualities are necessary for true friendship to exist? Circle the five most important qualities. Then compare with a partner.

acceptance	fun	kindness	maturity	sincerity
caring	generosity	love	modesty	trust
commitment	honesty	loyalty	sensitivity	understanding

In my opinion, the most important quality for a friendship is honesty.

C Listen Donna, Greg, and Sophia are talking about their best friends. How did they meet? What do they like about their friends? Take notes. ✳

	How did they meet?	**What do they like about their friends?**
Donna	*lived in the same building*	
Greg		
Sophia		

D Group work Discuss these questions.
- How did you meet your best friend? How long have you known each other?
- What qualities do you admire in your best friend?
- What is the best piece of advice a friend has ever given you?

I met my best friend in elementary school. We've known each other for . . .

Activity 2 **A Pair work** Look at the pictures. Imagine these people are friends of yours. What would you say to them? Write your ideas on a separate piece of paper.

① *Could you lend me some money?*

② *I have some good news and some bad news.*

③ *I just want to say how sorry I am.*

④ *Why didn't you call me when you said you would?*

B Listen 🎧 Now you will hear the conversations. Fill in what was actually said.

C Pair work Act out the conversations using your own ideas or those in part B.

Activity 3 **A Pair work** Read these quotes about friendship. Then discuss the questions below.

> "It's the friends you can call up at 4 A.M. that matter."
> *Marlene Dietrich*

> "Have no friends not equal to yourself."
> *Confucius*

> "Friends are born, not made."
> *Henry Adams*

> "A friend to all is a friend to none."
> *Aristotle*

> "Friendship with oneself is all-important because without it, one cannot be friends with anyone else in the world."
> *Eleanor Roosevelt*

> "Friendship is always a sweet responsibility, never an opportunity."
> *Kahlil Gibran*

- What do the quotes mean? Can you say them in a different way?
- Do you disagree with any of the quotes? Why?

B Pair work Tell a story about a friend using one of the quotes.

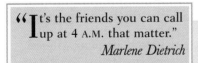

I once couldn't sleep at night because I was upset. I called my best friend and . . .

C Group work What best sums up your own feelings on friendship? Write one original quote, and then discuss it with your group.

Activity 1   **A   Pair work**   Imagine you are looking for a love match. Read the advertisement for a dating service, and complete the questionnaire. Then discuss the questions below.

Everyone can find Love

But if you can't . . . don't worry – just fill in the questionnaire below, and we will find your perfect partner.

1. How would you describe your personality?

- ☐ adventurous
- ☐ considerate
- ☐ conventional
- ☐ humorous
- ☐ mature
- ☐ practical
- ☐ reliable
- ☐ romantic
- ☐ serious
- ☐ shy
- ☐ sincere
- ☐ warmhearted

2. What kind of partner are you looking for?

Age:	min. _____	max. _____	☐ don't care
Height:	min. _____	max. _____	☐ don't care
Nationality:	_____		☐ don't care
Blood type:	_____		☐ don't care
Zodiac sign:	_____		☐ don't care

3. What personality traits are important to you in a partner?

_____   _____   _____

- What other information would you want to know before agreeing to meet someone for the first time?
- Which of the information above is the most important in choosing a partner?
- Were you totally honest answering the questions?

> I would also want to know if we have similar interests.

B   Pair work   Imagine your partner just had either the perfect date or the worst date ever. Ask your partner these questions, and think of your own.
- Who did you have a date with?
- Did you ask the person out on a date, or did the person ask you?
- Were you and your date alone, or did friends join you?
- What did you do? Who paid?

> Who did you have a date with?

> It was with my sister's best friend. We had a terrible time.

A Pair work Read these sentences. What do you think the highlighted expressions mean? After you've discussed the vocabulary, answer the questions below.

1. Janet and I are just friends. We have a platonic relationship.
2. When I was young, I had the biggest crush on a Hollywood actor.
3. They're too young to be in a serious relationship. It's just a case of puppy love.
4. You shouldn't flirt with other people when you're on a date.
5. If you're not compatible with your partner, the relationship will never work.
6. I got all dressed up for my date, and then he had the nerve to stand me up.

- Have you ever had a crush on someone? Who was it? What happened?
- Have you ever experienced puppy love?
- What makes two people compatible?
- Have you ever been stood up by a friend or a date? How did you feel?

> *I once had a crush on one of my classmates. One day I told . . .*

B Listen 🎧 Heather and George are talking about what happened to their classmates from high school. Use the symbols to indicate the relationships.

A↔B A and B like each other.	A→B A likes B, but B doesn't like A.
A = B A and B are married.	A ≠ B A and B are not together anymore.

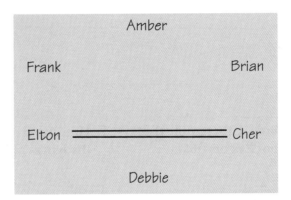

C Group work What advice is important to follow to have a healthy relationship? Choose the statement that you feel most strongly about, and discuss in a group.

Treat your partner the way you want your partner to treat you.

Ask a lot of questions before you get too involved.

Don't show how you feel. Play hard to get.

Be emotionally generous with everyone you meet.

Judge people not by the size of their bank accounts, but by the size of their hearts.

Don't play games – be yourself from the beginning.

> *I think you have to ask a lot of questions before you get too involved, or there may be surprises later.*

Review puzzles

Puzzle A

Use the clues to complete the puzzle with words from Unit 9.

Across

1. a sport for people who like water
2. I find it hard to .... when there's a lot of noise.
3. .... deeply – it'll help you relax.
4. Been sitting too long? Stand up and .... .
5. You can do exercises here.
6. .... techniques help to relieve stress.
7. a treatment based on pleasant smells
8. This kind of exercise is good for your heart.
9. Taking extra .... C may help you resist colds.
10. a treatment that uses needles
11. .... is quicker than walking.
12. the number of hours of sleep you should try to get

Down

13. Feeling stressed? Maybe it's because you .... !

13
1 | s | w | i | m | m | i | n | g |
2
3
4
5
6
7
8
9
10
11
12

Puzzle B

1. Here are 6 scrambled words. Unscramble the letters to make words from Lesson 10A.

ribaldzz	b _l i z z a r d_
hurtdog	d _ _ _ _ _ _ _
drylizz	(d) _ _ _ _ _ _
moderntruths	t _ _ _ _ _ ◯ _ _ _ _ _ _
hotpony	t _ _ _ _ _ _ _
tinglingh	l _ _ _ _ ◯ _ _ _

2. Here are 6 more scrambled words. Unscramble the letters to make words from Lesson 10B.

icevat	a _c t i v e_
routepin	e _ _ _ _ ◯ _ _
textnic	e _ _ _ _ ◯ _
gamma	m ◯ _ _ _
darntom	d _ _ _ _ _ _
yesreg	g _◯_ _ _

3. Now use the letters in the circles above to complete the sentence.

" _ _ _ _   _ _ _ , isn't it?"

Puzzle C

There are 19 words from Unit 11 in this word search puzzle. How many can you find? They all have something to do with THE NEWS.

```
J S A R T I C L E S E P E D S
O H T J B H R R A D Y K R J U
U E C O C H Z S N C E W N X V
R A P O R C N P C R W E M T I
N D R U R Y O L H I I A P P U
A L E C B R C R O T T T O A C
L I V P L L E U R I N H L P O
I N I B U O I S Z C E E I A L
S E E O I D R S P L S R T R U
T U W I S K L D H O S K I A M
Y X R E P O R T E R N H C Z N
D K N M A G A Z I N E D S Z I
M M A X D I S A S T E R E I S
I N T E R V I E W Q I O U N T
C E L E B R I T Y I M R U M T
```

Puzzle D

Use the clues to solve the puzzle with words from Unit 12.

Across

4. the opposite of "arrogance"
6. preferring not to behave in an unusual way
9. Friends have to be able to .... each other.
10. to be playfully romantic
11. when a couple goes out together
12. Sending your partner flowers is a .... gesture.
14. He makes me laugh; he's .... to be with.
15. If two people are a good match, they are .... .

Down

1. kind and friendly
2. the opposite of "silly"
3. taking risks and living a little dangerously
5. When people get married, they make a .... to be together.
7. faithfulness
8. the opposite of "selfishness"
13. When he was young, he had a .... on his teacher.

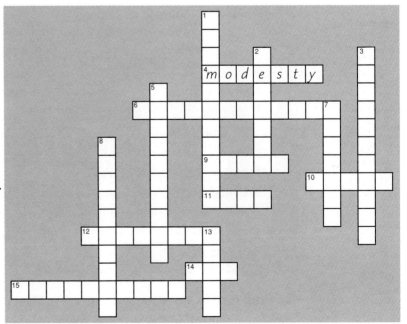

13A Please be careful!

A Read/listen 🎧 First read the advice for people who are going hiking in the mountains, and try to guess the missing words. Then listen and check your answers.

HIKING IN THE MOUNTAINS—SOME DOS AND DON'TS

Precautions

1. Have at least _____ people in your party. Don't go hiking _____ .

2. Expect the weather to get worse. Don't rely completely on weather _____ .

3. Allow yourself plenty of _____ . Don't let darkness catch up with you.

4. Walk at the pace of the _____ member of your group. Don't leave anyone _____ .

5. Tell people where you're going _____ you start off. Don't _____ to tell them when you get back.

Equipment

6. _____ your route before you set off. Take a _____ and a _____ so that you know where you are at all times.

7. Carry some _____ , waterproof clothing in your backpack, and remember to take a first-aid _____ .

8. Wear proper hiking _____ – not sneakers or sandals.

9. Put emergency rations in your _____ , like chocolate, dried fruit, and water, as well as any sandwiches and drinks you need during the day.

10. Pack a _____ in case you get caught in the dark.

B Pair work Compare your answers. Then discuss these questions.
- What additional advice can you give?
- Is there any advice you think is unimportant?
- Would you enjoy hiking in the mountains? Why or why not?

I'd recommend taking a cell phone in case there's an emergency.

Activity 2   **A Pair work** Look at the pictures. What advice would you give to the people in these situations? Write your ideas on a separate piece of paper.

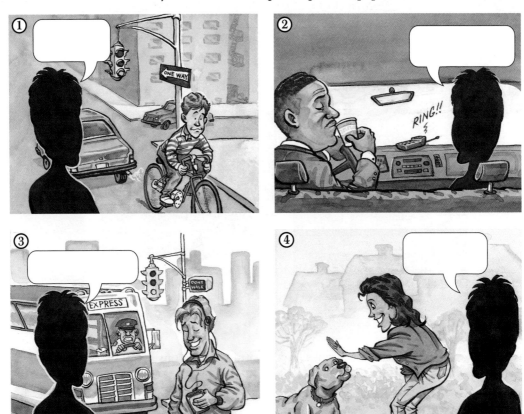

B Listen 🎧 Now you will hear the conversations. Fill in what was actually said.

C Pair work Act out the conversations using your own ideas or those in part B.

Activity 3   **A Pair work** Choose one of these activities. Make a list of safety rules.

bicycling

snowboarding

rock climbing

swimming

jogging

camping

Activity:	
Dos	**Don'ts**

B Join another pair Look at each other's safety rules. Do you agree with them?

I agree that people should wear a helmet when bicycling, but I don't think that . . .

13B Exciting – or dangerous?

A **Pair work** Look at these photos. Then discuss the questions below.

- Which of these activities look exciting, dangerous, or both?
- Which of the things above would you try? Why?
- What is the riskiest thing you've ever done? What happened?

> *I think the safari looks both exciting and dangerous.*

B **Pair work** How much of a risk taker are you? Interview your partner.

Do you . . . ?	Never	Sometimes	Usually	Always
1. listen to the weather forecast before going out	☐	☐	☐	☐
2. buy lottery tickets	☐	☐	☐	☐
3. back up your computer data	☐	☐	☐	☐
4. take a map when you visit a new place	☐	☐	☐	☐
5. ride a motorcycle	☐	☐	☐	☐
6. write out a list before going shopping	☐	☐	☐	☐
7. walk home alone late at night	☐	☐	☐	☐
8. lock the front door to your house	☐	☐	☐	☐
9. always plan what you'll do the next day	☐	☐	☐	☐
10. wear a seat belt	☐	☐	☐	☐

C **Join another pair** Turn to page 89 to calculate your score. Tell your partner the results, and discuss the questions.
- Do you agree with your evaluation? Why or why not?
- Which behaviors are risky and should be avoided? Which are commonsense actions that anyone should take?
- Are you an adventurous person overall, or do you tend to avoid taking risks?

A Pair work Read what the people below say about why they take risks. Which of these words best describe them? Which describe qualities an adventurous person should have?

arrogant	confident	determined	experienced	persistent
brave	curious	enthusiastic	modest	physically fit

Lea
"I take risks all the time. I'm strong and not afraid of life. I can do anything."

Thomas
"Many people say I'm adventurous. I don't know if that's true, but I do like to try new things."

Elaine
"Risk taking makes me feel really alive. I learn a lot about the world, too."

B Listen 🎧 Jane, Tony, and Mary are talking about frightening experiences they have had. Complete the chart. ✳

	What happened?	Why was he/she frightened?	Did it end happily?
Jane	snake crawled over foot		
Tony			
Mary			

C Pair work Compare your answers. Then discuss these questions.
- Have you ever been in a similar situation? What happened?
- What was one of your greatest adventures?
- What adventurous thing would you like to try someday?

D Group work Rank these activities from 1 to 6 (1 = easiest for me to do, 6 = hardest for me to do). Then discuss the questions.

	take a trip without planning an itinerary		sing in front of a large audience
	quit your job		not see a dentist for several years
	tell someone you have a crush on him or her		ride on an upside-down roller coaster

- Which activity would be the hardest for you? the easiest? Why?
- Which of these have you done? What happened?
- What are some possible negative consequences of doing these activities?
- Are there any positive consequences of doing them?

It would be hard for me to quit my job, because I'm someone who needs security.

14A How to be popular

A Pair work Look at these photos. Then discuss the questions below.

- What do you think these people are talking about?
- When you are getting to know someone, what qualities make a good impression?

B Pair work These words can describe someone who doesn't make a good impression. Circle the words below that you don't know, and ask your partner to explain them. Use a dictionary to look up any that neither of you knows.

arrogant	complaining	condescending	rude	superficial
cold	conceited	irritable	stubborn	whiny

C Listen 🎧 You will hear four conversations. Choose the word or words that best describe the impression the second speaker makes. Then compare your answers with a partner.

1. *whiny*_____   3. _____
2. _____   4. _____

D Group work How important are these qualities in making a good impression? Write ✔✔ (very important), ✔ (important), or ✗ (not important) next to each item. Then compare with your group.

...... **ability to listen**	...... **friendliness**	...... **appearance**
...... **confidence**	...... **intelligence**	...... **sincerity**
...... **sense of fashion**	...... **good manners**	...... **pleasing voice**

I don't think intelligence and a sense of fashion are important.

But a sense of fashion is part of your appearance. If you don't dress . . .

Activity 2   **A Pair work** Are you a good conversationalist? Take this quiz together to find out. Give each item a number from 1 to 5.

1 = never   2 = hardly ever   3 = sometimes   4 = often   5 = all the time

Are you a good conversationalist?

Before or during a conversation, do you . . . ?

1. ask questions ☐
2. talk about a wide range of topics ☐
3. encourage others to speak ☐
4. avoid interrupting people ☐
5. plan ahead what you're going to say ☐
6. exaggerate or embellish stories ☐
7. try to make others laugh ☐
8. listen carefully ☐
9. tell funny or interesting stories ☐

That reminds me of another joke. Wait,... let's see, how does it go...?

B Pair work Add up the numbers, and look at page 90 for an evaluation of your score. Then discuss the questions.
- Which of the questions in the quiz are a good way of judging conversational skills?
- Do any questions seem silly or irrelevant? If so, which ones?
- What else is necessary to do to be a good conversationalist?

It's very important to ask questions to show you're interested, but not so important to . . .

C Join another pair Look at these conversation topics. Circle the five that you like to talk about the most. Then discuss the questions below.

books	food	politics	school	TV shows
computers	gossip	private matters	shopping	vacations
dating	movies	relationships	sports	the weather
family	news events	religion	travel	work

- Which topics do you like to talk about? What other topics do you like to discuss?
- What do you generally avoid discussing? Why?
- Are there any topics that are inappropriate in your culture?
- Which topics would be appropriate for school? the office? with friends? with parents?
- Which ones would be inappropriate for those situations?

My friends and I like to talk about topics that relate to us, like dating, school, and sports. We don't like . . .

D Communication task 🎭 Work in groups of three. One of you should look at Task 13 on page 78, one at Task 29 on page 83, and one at Task 35 on page 85. You're going to practice telling each other some jokes and funny stories.

14B Managing your life

Activity 1 **A Pair work** Look at these people at their desks at work. Who do you think is the best employee? Why?

Sarah

Hank

Amanda

> I think Sarah is the best employee. She's talking on the phone and looks busy.

B Listen 🎧 You will hear three conversations about the situations in part A. Take notes on what the people are talking about. Now who do you think is the best employee?

Sarah	
Hank	
Amanda	

C Pair work How important for success are these qualities? Write ✔✔ (very important), ✔ (important), or ✗ (not important) next to each item.

☐ a practical mind	☐ the ability to write well	☐ the ability to "think on your feet"
☐ concentration	☐ being good at flattery	☐ popularity with colleagues
☐ physical fitness	☐ a willingness to learn	☐ accepting responsibility
☐ patience	☐ being adaptable	☐ being good with numbers
☐ ambition	☐ a good family background	☐ the ability to work under pressure
☐ ruthlessness	☐ willingness to take risks	☐ being good at giving orders
☐ a good education	☐ the ability to delegate	☐ the ability to express yourself

D Group work Compare your answers. Give reasons for your choices.

> A good education is very important.

> It's important, but there are many people without a good education who are successful. It's more important to . . .

Activity 2 | **A Pair work** Read these items from *Life's Little Instruction Book* by H. Jackson Brown Jr. Check (✔) the three most helpful pieces of advice for how people should lead their lives.

.... Admit your mistakes.

.... Practice empathy. Try to see things from other points of view.

.... Don't allow the phone to interrupt important moments.

.... Don't be afraid to say, "I don't know."

.... Give people a second chance, but not a third.

.... Hear both sides before judging.

.... Don't be afraid to say, "I need help."

.... Be a good loser.

.... Learn to show enthusiasm, even when you don't feel like it.

B Group work Compare your answers. Then discuss these questions.
- Is there any advice you all find helpful?
- What advice did your parents give you? your grandparents? your teachers?
- If you could give people only one piece of advice about how to lead their lives, what would it be?

We all think it's helpful to hear both sides of a story before judging.

Yes, it's very important to be fair.

C Listen 🎧 You will hear four people talking about what they'd like to accomplish in life. Write down what each person wants to do. Then discuss the questions. ✳

Tom	
Antonio	
Young-Joon	
Marianne	

- Which person do you think has the most interesting idea?
- Do you want to do any of the same things?

D Work alone Below is another piece of advice from *Life's Little Instruction Book*.

> Make a list of 25 things you want to experience.
> Carry it in your wallet, and refer to it often.

Begin your own list in class. Write ten things you want to do. You can finish the list at home.

E Group work Share your list with your group members.

Activity 1 **A Pair work** Look at these photos. Then discuss the questions below.

- What are these people doing? Where do you think they are?
- What are the advantages and disadvantages of each way of traveling?
- Which similar experiences have you had? Which activity looks most interesting?

B Listen 🎧 Two tourist groups are preparing to go on a day trip with their guides. First read the questions they ask. Then listen and write the answers. ✳

Questions	Tour 1	Tour 2
How many will be in my group?		
What do I need to bring?		
What will we do in the morning?		
What will we have for lunch?		
What will we do in the afternoon?		
What extra costs will there be?		

C Pair work Compare your answers. Which tour sounds more interesting?

D Group work Think of a trip you have taken recently. Tell your group about it.

> *I went to the beach with some friends. Everything was going well until . . .*

A Read/listen 🎧 First read the tips for first-time visitors to Australia, and try to guess the missing words. Then listen and check your answers.

> • Make sure you get a _____ before entering the country. Every traveler to Australia must have one.
> • Buy a _____ and find out as much about the country as you can.
> • Stay in Australian youth _____; they're cheap and a great way to meet other _____.
> • To save money, buy a long-distance _____.
> • Bring _____ clothes if you're traveling there between the months of November and March.
> • Don't walk _____ because there are a lot of poisonous _____ and spiders there.
> • The Australian sun is very strong. For protection, remember the slogan "Slip, slop, slap": Slip on a _____, slop on _____, and slap on a _____.

B Pair work Compare your answers. Would you like to visit Australia?

C Pair work Read these general travel tips. Which do you think are practical? Which couldn't you follow?

Flying	Hotels	Safety
• Avoid delays by flying early in the day. • Choose nonstop flights. This will lessen the risk of lost luggage. • Avoid coffee and tea. Instead, drink fruit juice and water. This will help reduce jet lag.	• Don't accept the first price offered. Always ask for a cheaper room. • Ask for the corporate rate, even if you don't work for a large company. They may give it to you. • If no rooms are available, call back after 6 P.M., when rooms reserved for "no-shows" become available.	• Don't rely on backpacks. They are easily accessed by pickpockets. • Be aware of overcharging for transportation from the airport to the city. • Don't keep all your cash and credit cards together in the same place. If you lose them, you're out of luck.

> *It's not practical to always fly early in the day.*

D Communication task 👥 Work with a partner. One of you should look at Task 14 on page 78, and the other at Task 30 on page 84. You're going to read some advice for traveling in a foreign area.

E Group work Imagine that a friend is planning a two-week trip to your country. What advice would you give in the following areas? Share your tips with the group.

driving	food and drink	packing	shopping	tours
entertainment	hotels	safety	tipping	transportation

> *I'd tell my friend to buy a rail pass. Traveling by train is . . .*

Activity 1 **A Work alone** What do you like to do on vacation? Check (✔) the five things you most like to do. Add three more to the list. Then compare with a partner.

- [ ] learn a language
- [ ] watch wildlife
- [ ] go hiking
- [ ] visit amusement parks
- [ ] go to a beach
- [ ] sunbathe

- [ ] see family
- [ ] meet local people
- [ ] try adventure sports
- [ ] go camping
- [ ] visit art museums
- [ ] shop

- [ ] try new foods
- [ ] go for quiet walks
- [ ] be alone
- ....
- ....
- ....

> *Believe it or not, when I go on vacation, I like to be alone.*

B Listen 🎧 You will hear two people talking about fantastic trips they remember. Number the pictures in each story from 1 to 4 in the order they happened.

C Pair work Compare your answers. What would you enjoy – and not enjoy – about these two trips?

> *The only thing I probably wouldn't enjoy about the first trip is the market. That's because I . . .*

D Communication task 👥 Work with a partner. One of you should look at Task 15 on page 78, and the other at Task 31 on page 84. You're going to have some additional pictures to describe.

A Pair work Read these two descriptions of vacations. Then discuss the questions below.

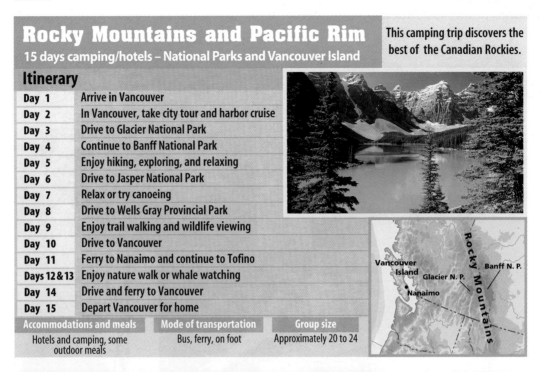

Rocky Mountains and Pacific Rim
15 days camping/hotels – National Parks and Vancouver Island

This camping trip discovers the best of the Canadian Rockies.

Itinerary

Day 1	Arrive in Vancouver
Day 2	In Vancouver, take city tour and harbor cruise
Day 3	Drive to Glacier National Park
Day 4	Continue to Banff National Park
Day 5	Enjoy hiking, exploring, and relaxing
Day 6	Drive to Jasper National Park
Day 7	Relax or try canoeing
Day 8	Drive to Wells Gray Provincial Park
Day 9	Enjoy trail walking and wildlife viewing
Day 10	Drive to Vancouver
Day 11	Ferry to Nanaimo and continue to Tofino
Days 12 & 13	Enjoy nature walk or whale watching
Day 14	Drive and ferry to Vancouver
Day 15	Depart Vancouver for home

Accommodations and meals	Mode of transportation	Group size
Hotels and camping, some outdoor meals	Bus, ferry, on foot	Approximately 20 to 24

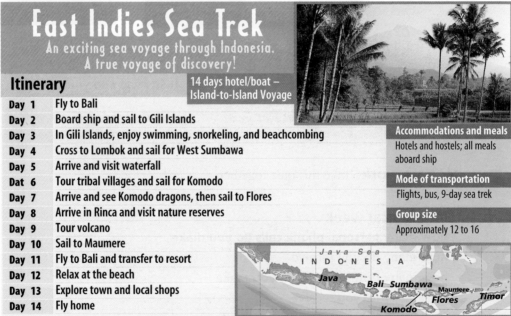

East Indies Sea Trek
An exciting sea voyage through Indonesia.
A true voyage of discovery!

Itinerary

14 days hotel/boat – Island-to-Island Voyage

Day 1	Fly to Bali
Day 2	Board ship and sail to Gili Islands
Day 3	In Gili Islands, enjoy swimming, snorkeling, and beachcombing
Day 4	Cross to Lombok and sail for West Sumbawa
Day 5	Arrive and visit waterfall
Dat 6	Tour tribal villages and sail for Komodo
Day 7	Arrive and see Komodo dragons, then sail to Flores
Day 8	Arrive in Rinca and visit nature reserves
Day 9	Tour volcano
Day 10	Sail to Maumere
Day 11	Fly to Bali and transfer to resort
Day 12	Relax at the beach
Day 13	Explore town and local shops
Day 14	Fly home

Accommodations and meals
Hotels and hostels; all meals aboard ship

Mode of transportation
Flights, bus, 9-day sea trek

Group size
Approximately 12 to 16

- Which of the two destinations would you choose? Why?
- What are the most attractive features of each one? What are some drawbacks?

B Pair work Choose a different destination, and design your own vacation brochure.

C Group work Share your brochure with your group. Imagine you are a travel agent, and "sell" the trip to some potential customers.

This trip would interest you if you want to try something totally different.

16A Using the phone

A Pair work Look at these photos. Then discuss the questions below.

- What do you think each person is saying?
- Would you use a cell phone in these situations? Why or why not?
- Do you have a cell phone? If not, why not? If so, when do you use it?

> I think the man in the first picture is talking about something personal.

> I think so, too. The other people in the elevator look annoyed.

B Pair work Take this quiz together.

In a typical week . . . ?	
how many personal phone calls do you make	
how many do you receive	
how many business calls do you make	
how many do you receive	
how many times do you use a cell phone	
how many times do you beep people	
how many times are you beeped	
how many times do you use a pay phone	
how many minutes does your average phone call last	

C Join another pair Compare your answers and discuss these questions.
- Who uses the phone the most?
- Do you want to change any of your phone habits?

Activity 2 **A Pair work** Look at these pictures. What would you say in these situations?
Write your ideas on a separate piece of paper.

B Listen Now you will hear the conversations. Fill in what was actually said.

C Pair work Act out the conversations using your own ideas or those in part B.

Activity 3 **A Listen** You will hear two phone messages. Write down the important information.

B Pair work Compare your notes with the model notes on page 90.

C Communication task Work with a partner. One of you should
look at Task 17 on page 79, and the other at Task 33 on page 85. You're going to
see some information to exchange in some phone calls.

16B The ideal job

A Pair work Who normally holds these jobs in your country? Write **W** for women, **M** for men, and **E** for either men or women.

...... schoolteacher	...... university professor	...... firefighter
...... taxi driver	...... politician	...... surgeon
...... newscaster	...... symphony conductor	...... receptionist
...... butcher	...... cashier	...... chef
...... company president	...... police officer	...... nurse

B Join another pair Compare your results. Then discuss these questions.
- What other jobs are typically done by men? typically done by women?
- Why do you think some jobs are most commonly done by one gender?
- Do you personally know any women who are doing a job typically done by men? men doing a job typically done by women? What challenges do they face?
- Are there any special advantages to being a female in the workforce in your country? What are the disadvantages?
- What are the pros and cons of being a male in the workforce in your country?

> Bus drivers are typically men.

> Artists are . . .

C Listen 🎧 Dr. Alexander, an expert on the brain, is giving a lecture. According to the research he quotes, who does better on the tasks? Write **M** for men and **W** for women. Do you agree with his ideas? ✳

...... rapid naming	...... map reading
...... remembering lists and stories	...... handling words and concepts
...... mathematics	...... recognizing patterns

D Class activity Try these two tests to see if Dr. Alexander's theories are true for your class.

> Spend one minute writing down as many synonyms for these words as you can:
> **good   bad**

> Spend one minute writing down as many words as you can that you associate with:
> **travel and tourism**

When you finish, count up the number of words. Do the women in your class have higher scores than the men? According to Dr. Alexander, they should.

Activity 2   **A**   **Pair work**   Look at these photos. Then discuss the questions below.

     lumberjack   comedian   pilot   soldier

- Which of these jobs would you most like to have? least like to have? Why?
- What are the advantages to doing each job? disadvantages?

B   **Group work**   Brainstorm as many jobs as you can for these categories. Think of a job for each category that would interest you, and explain why.

jobs with an element of danger   jobs that require a creative mind
jobs that use a foreign language   jobs that are performed outdoors
jobs that require an analytical mind   jobs that can be done from home

> *I would be interested in being a flight attendant because I would have a chance to use my English.*

C   **Pair work**   Which items below would be important to you on a job? Write ✔✔ (very important), ✔ (important), or ✗ (not important) next to each item.

.... **getting increased responsibility**	.... **working independently**
.... **earning plenty of money**	.... **having financial security**
.... **being asked for advice**	.... **solving problems**
.... **winning the praise of superiors**	.... **exercising power**
.... **helping others**	.... **learning new things**
.... **getting promoted**	.... **seeing results**
.... **feeling successful**	.... **being part of a team**
.... **working under pressure**	.... **being popular with coworkers**
.... **gaining respect of colleagues**	.... **having comfortable working conditions**

D   **Join another pair**   Compare your results. Then discuss these questions.
- What job would you recommend for each person in your group?
- What job would you definitely not recommend?
- If you could have any job in the world, what would it be? Why?

> *. . . could be a surgeon.*

> *Being part of a team and helping others are important to her.*

Review puzzles

Puzzle A

Use the clues to complete the puzzle with words from Unit 13.

Across

1. You won't get lost if you have one of these.
2. If something scary happens, you feel .... .
3. unsafe
4. what happens as a result
5. An .... person has done many things.
6. Don't forget to .... up your computer data.
7. Not wearing a .... belt in a car is unsafe.
8. A dangerous sport in the mountains is rock .... .
9. the most dangerous mode of transportation?
10. If you have an .... for a trip, you know where and when you're going.
11. sure of yourself
12. Do you make a .... before you go to the store?
13. Buy a ticket for this and hope you win!

Down

14. With adventurous sports you need to be ....

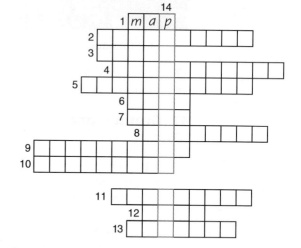

Puzzle B

1. Here are 6 scrambled words. Unscramble the letters to make words from Lesson 14A.

braput   a _b_ _r_ _u_ _p_ _t_
bobturns   (s)_ _ _ _ ◯_ _
organrat   a _ _ _ _ _ _ _ _
carefulispi   s _ _ _ _ _ ◯_ _ _ _
inwhy   w _ _ _ _
campinglion   c _ _◯_ _ _ _ _ _

2. Here are 6 more scrambled words. Unscramble the letters to make words from Lesson 14B.

badpalate   a _d_ _a_ _p_ _t_ _a_ _b_ _l_ _e_
assumethin   e◯_ _ _ _ _ _ _ _◯_
seepurrs   p _ _ _◯_ _ _
ledgetea   d◯_ _ _ _ _ _
oilypuprat   p _ _ _ _ _ ◯_ _ _
sellingwins   w◯_ _ _ _ _ _ _ _

3. Now use the letters in the circles above to complete the sentence.

"It's important to make a good first _ _ _ _ _ _ _ _ _ _ ."

Puzzle C

There are 17 words from Unit 15 in this word search puzzle. How many can you find? They all have something to do with TRAVEL and TOURISM.

Puzzle D

Use the clues to solve the puzzle with words from Unit 16.

Across

1. I'm afraid she's not here. Can I take a .... ?
3. He or she is elected.
4. A soldier belongs to this.
6. He or she works in a store.
9. It's important to have comfortable working .... .
13. a group of people who work closely together
15. all the people who work

Down

2. the money you get paid each month
5. admiration
6. someone you work with
7. He or she flies an airplane.
8. another word for someone you work with
10. He or she works in a hospital.
11. Job .... means not having to worry that you'll get fired.
12. getting a better job in the same company
14. the reason why most people work

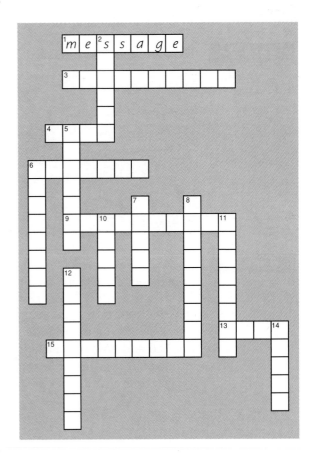

Communication tasks

Task 1

Complete the puzzle below. Follow these instructions: There are eight rooms and eight tenants at Sunshine Apartments. You know that the eight tenants are Brian, David, Etsuko, Fran, Craig, Alberto, Hannah, and Gina. You don't know their exact apartment numbers.

You have three clues, and your partner has three different clues. Take turns telling each other your clues. Write each person's name in the correct room.

Sunshine Apartments

Room 201	Room 202	Room 203	Room 204
Room 101	**Room 102** *Fran*	**Room 103**	**Room 104**

1. Fran is in Room 102.

2. Hannah is immediately below David.

What does your first clue say?

3. Brian is between Alberto and Craig.

Which is Gina's apartment? Turn to page 90 to check your answers.

Task 2

Here are some more detailed clues about John.

Task 3

Interview your partner, who has just walked the full length of your country to raise money for charity. First think about some questions you're going to ask.

Now it's your turn to be interviewed. You have just been rescued after spending a year alone on a tropical island. Think about and write down some experiences you had and how you managed to survive. You are happy to be home again, but during your year on the island, you got very used to living alone. It will be hard for you to live with other people again after so long on your own.

Task 4 Look at this cartoon strip, and figure out what happened. Tell the story as if it happened to a friend of a friend.

You'll never believe what happened to a friend of a friend.

Now listen to your partner's story. Ask questions to get additional details.

Task 5 Here are some more learning tips to share with your partner. Which do you both think are useful? Which are less useful?

1. To help you remember English vocabulary, highlight the new words you want to remember.
2. Keep a vocabulary notebook with a new page for each different topic.
3. When using a dictionary, look at the examples – not just the definitions.
4. Rewrite notes to help you remember information you need for an exam.
5. If you write an essay in an exam, don't just write the first thing that comes into your head – write a plan first.
6. When writing an essay, leave some space between each paragraph so there's room to add an extra sentence later.

Task 6 Read this information about Martha Stewart. Try to memorize the main points, and then share the story with your partner. Don't read the text out loud.

Martha Kostyra was born in a working-class community near New York City, on August 3, 1941. During college, she met Andy Stewart, and the two married in 1961. After moving to the country, Martha started a catering business in the late 1970s. She soon became known for her gourmet menus and unique, creative presentation. Within a decade, Martha Stewart, Inc., had grown into a $1 million business.

Stewart then expanded into the world of publishing with a series of best-selling books. However, her newfound fame took its toll on her personal life, as her marriage ended in divorce in 1990. In the early 1990s, her lifestyle empire grew to include two magazines, a cable television show, a newspaper column, a radio show, an Internet site, and $763 million in annual retail sales. In 1999, she saw her company go public. Stewart herself controls 96 percent of the voting shares in her company and is now worth $1.2 billion.

Now find out about Jean Paul Getty from your partner. Are there any similarities between their two lives?

Explain to your partner how to draw a continuous line to create this drawing.

First, draw a straight line from 5 to 24. Then continue from 24 to E. When you get to E, draw a line up to 5. Next, ...

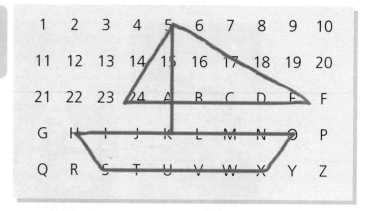

Carefully study these instructions together before you rejoin the group.

How to make yogurt

Boil milk for one minute.

Leave milk to cool to body temperature.

Mix in some yogurt to act as a starter.

Pour into a jar and cover loosely.

Put it in a warm place until morning.

The next morning, you'll have yogurt!

Put it in the refrigerator to chill.

Serve with honey, nuts, or fruit. Enjoy!

Explain to the other members of the group how to make yogurt.

Read the news story, and then close your book. Try to retell the story in your own words. Do not read the stories aloud to each other.

Better Safe than Sorry

Chrysanthemum Choo, of Miami, is probably the world's safest driver. Ms. Choo, 30, had returned to her car after shopping. She started the engine and patiently waited for an opportunity to drive out onto the main road. Eight hours later, she was still waiting. "I like to be careful," she explained. Things became quieter during the night, but unfortunately by then, Ms. Choo had fallen asleep. She awoke the next morning just in time for rush hour. Four hours later, she finally saw her chance and sped out onto the road – straight into the side of a police car. "I obviously wasn't careful enough," she admitted.

Task 10 *The Little Book of Calm* by Paul Wilson has advice for people who are feeling stressed. Study these tips and explain them to your partner in your own words.

Waste some time
Hardworking people never waste time on frivolous, fun-filled activities. Yet, for hardworking people, *any* time spent this way is far from wasted.

Start ten minutes early
Start every journey ten minutes early. Not only will you avoid the stress of haste, but if all goes well, you'll have ten minutes to relax before your next engagement.

Task 11 Study these instructions and then explain to your partner how to do the exercises.

Exercises for the arms

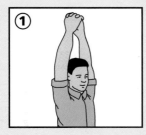 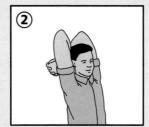 

① Link your fingers and hands in front of your chest. Lift your hands and arms up above your head. Reach for the roof. Breathe in deeply. Hold for three seconds. **②** Now, with your arms raised, bend your arms at elbows, and bring them down behind your head. Breathe out. Hold for three seconds. **③** Then straighten your arms, and stretch your hands up again. Breathe in. Hold for three seconds. Bend and stretch three times.

Task 12 Look at this picture, and discuss the questions below. Then join another pair, and tell them about your picture.

- Who are the people? What is their relationship to each other?
- Where are they? What are they doing?
- What do you think happened before this? What is going to happen next?
- What is the story behind the picture?

Task 13 Memorize the main points and the punch line in these funny stories and jokes. Then take turns telling them to your group. Try to make a good impression by telling them in a lively and interesting way.

> A woman was stopped by a police officer for driving too fast.
> **Police officer:** Why were you speeding, ma'am?
> **Woman:** My brakes are bad, so I wanted to get home before I had an accident.

> A man stopped a taxi and spoke to the driver.
> **Man:** How much to take me to the train station?
> **Driver:** About $20, sir.
> **Man:** And how much for my suitcase?
> **Driver:** No charge for the suitcase, sir.
> **Man:** OK, just take the suitcase. I'll walk.

Now discuss these questions.
- Who do you think is the best at telling jokes and stories? Why?
- What other funny stories do you know?

Task 14 Read these tips for travelers, and try to remember the main points. Then tell your partner the tips in your own words.

Dress awareness	**Transportation**	**Food and drink**
At home, you wouldn't go to the supermarket in your swimsuit, but some people think it's OK to do this when on vacation. Remember, in some societies, walking around in shorts and T-shirts is very offensive. Use common sense.	Consider making your own travel arrangements locally. Independent travel may take more organization, but the effort can be well rewarded. Local guides will know the area well, and by using their services, you will be providing income and employment to local people.	If you only eat in your hotel, the local people are unlikely to benefit. Try local food and drinks. This will benefit the local economy and allow you to try something new. You may wish to stick to bottled water, though.

Task 15 Look at these pictures that show different events from the same trip. Imagine that these things happened to you.

First find out about your partner's trip. Then tell your partner about your trip.

> It was an interesting vacation because I . . .

Task 16

Complete the puzzle below. Follow these instructions: There are eight rooms and eight tenants at Sunshine Apartments. You know that the eight tenants are Brian, David, Etsuko, Fran, Craig, Alberto, Hannah, and Gina. You don't know their exact apartment numbers.

You have three clues, and your partner has three different clues. Take turns telling each other your clues. Write each person's name in the correct room.

Sunshine Apartments

Room 201	Room 202	Room 203	Room 204
_____	_____	_____	_____

Room 101	Room 102	Room 103	Room 104
_____	*Fran*	_____	_____

1. Hannah is two rooms to the right of Fran.

My first clue says that Hannah is . . .

2. Craig is immediately to the left of David.

3. Etsuko is not below Craig.

Which is Gina's apartment? Turn to page 90 to check your answers.

Task 17

You're going to call your partner. Sit back-to-back so that you use only your voices to communicate. Follow the instructions below. Leave messages using your own name.

You want to speak to Beth Martin.
You're calling to let her know you're arriving tomorrow evening at 6:45 on Flight KL 406 from San Francisco.
You want Beth to meet you at the airport.

You want to speak to Mr. D.H. McClean.
You're calling because there is a problem with a purchase order. The number is DXH03-2881-MX.
You want him to check the order. You will call back tomorrow morning.

When you finish, your partner will ask to speak to two people. They are not available. Take the messages.

Message 1

Message 2

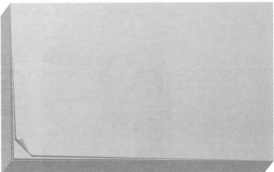

Task 18   Here are some more detailed clues about John.

Task 19   Look at this picture, and discuss the questions below. Then join another pair, and tell them about your picture.

- What is the animal doing? Why?
- Who is the woman?
- What do you think happened before this? What is going to happen next?
- What is the story behind the picture?

Task 20   Listen to your partner's story. Ask questions to get additional details.

Then look at this cartoon strip, and figure out what happened. Tell the story as if it happened to a friend of a friend.

You'll never believe what happened to a friend of a friend.

Task 21 Here are some more learning tips to share with your partner. Which do you both think are useful? Which are less useful?

1. When you come across a new word you want to remember, "make up" a sentence using it and write it down.
2. Many words are used to talk about all kinds of topics. Write new words on the blank pages at the beginning of your notebook.
3. Use colored markers in your notes, and highlight the important points.
4. Work with another student to practice speaking English together before an oral exam.
5. Get a good night's sleep, and have a good breakfast before an exam.
6. When writing an essay, leave a wide margin so there is room to make minor changes later.

Task 22 Find out about Martha Stewart from your partner.
Now read this information about Jean Paul Getty. Try to memorize the main points, and then share the story with your partner. Don't read the text aloud.

Jean Paul Getty was born on December 15, 1892, in Minneapolis, Minnesota. He took after his father and was a success in the oil business. By the age of 23, Jean Paul had made his first $1 million. During the Depression of the 1930s, he built an empire by buying other oil companies.

Although Getty was one of the richest men in the world and owned houses in England and California, he lived most of his life in hotel rooms. His hobbies were making money and collecting works of art. His wonderful collection can be seen at the Getty Museum in Malibu, California, which opened in 1974. He published several books, including *My Life and Fortunes* and *How to Be Rich*. He died in 1976, worth over $1 billion.

Are there any similarities between their two lives?

Task 23 Explain to your partner how to draw a continuous line to create this drawing.

First, draw a straight line from 15 to 17. Then continue from 17 to 8. When you get to 8, draw a line to 7. Next, . . .

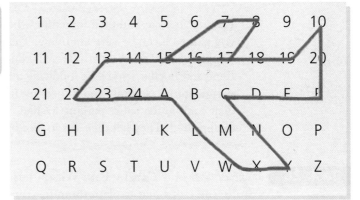

Task 24   Carefully study these instructions together before you rejoin the group.

How to repair a scratched CD

 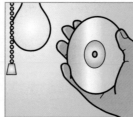 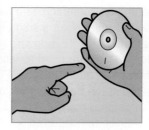 

Find a CD that always skips while playing.

Hold the CD up to a bright light.

Look for scratch on bottom side of CD.

Put small amount of toothpaste on a cloth.

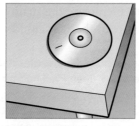 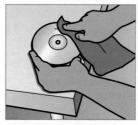 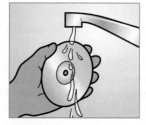 

Place CD onto a flat, clean surface.

Polish the CD until scratch disappears.

Clean with water and dry completely.

Insert CD into player, and enjoy the music!

Explain to the other members of the group how to repair a scratched CD.

Task 25   Read the news story, and then close your book. Try to retell the story in your own words. Do not read the stories aloud to each other.

The Disappearing Parking Lot

Parking your car and then forgetting where you parked it can be very annoying. This is what happened to an elderly French couple, René and Lucille Schubelle, following a recent shopping trip. Not only could they not find their car, but the entire parking lot had disappeared! They left their car in a parking lot in Calais, France. Two hours later, they returned to find the lot had vanished. They contacted the police, who discovered that the Schubelles had parked their car on the deck of a ferry bound for Dover, England, 25 miles across the English Channel.

Task 26   *The Little Book of Calm* by Paul Wilson has advice for people who are feeling stressed. Study these tips and explain them to your partner in your own words.

Listen for the quiet
Quiet is the essence of calm. You cannot *force* quiet; you can only accept it when it comes. But if you listen for it, really listen, you will find it in the most unexpected places. All it takes is a little concentration.

Wear comfortable shoes
Any reflexologist will tell you that true relaxation begins at the feet. It seems obvious, but wearing comfortable shoes is nearly as relaxing as wearing no shoes at all.

Task 27 Study these instructions and then explain to your partner how to do the exercises.

Exercises for the lower back, legs, and feet

① ② ③ ④

① Start with your feet flat on the floor. Raise your heels as high as you can. Hold for three seconds. ② Lower your heel to the floor, and raise your toes off the ground. Hold for three seconds. Repeat five times with each foot. ③ Next, lift your foot and straighten your leg. Hold for three seconds. ④ Then point your foot down, clenching toes, keeping your leg straight. Hold for three seconds. Repeat five times with each foot.

Task 28 You are going to be interviewed. You have just walked the full length of your country to raise money for charity. Think about and write down some experiences you had in the different cities and regions you walked through. You feel very tired but proud because you raised a lot of money.

Now you are going to interview your partner, who has just been rescued after spending a year alone on a tropical island. Think about some questions you're going to ask.

Task 29 Memorize the main points and the punch line in these funny stories and jokes. Then take turns telling them to your group. Try to make a good impression by telling them in a lively and interesting way.

Mr. and Mrs. Brown got to the airport just before their flight to New York.

Mrs. Brown: Well, we made it, dear.
Mr. Brown: Yes, but I wish we'd brought the piano with us.
Mrs. Brown: What on earth for?
Mr. Brown: Because I left our tickets on it.

Mrs. Harris and Mrs. Greene are having coffee.

Mrs. Greene: I hope you don't mind my asking, but how old are you?
Mrs. Harris: I'm 39, but I don't look it, do I?
Mrs. Greene: No, but you *used* to.

Now discuss these questions.
- Who do you think is the best at telling jokes and stories? Why?
- What other funny stories do you know?

Task 30

Read these tips for travelers, and try to remember the main points. Then tell your partner the tips in your own words.

Shopping	**Making friends**	**Photography**
If you buy all your souvenirs in your hotel, the local craftspeople who made them won't see much of the profit. Shop at local markets, and buy directly from the craftspeople. Check that the souvenirs you buy will not damage the environment.	Learning some of the local language, such as "please," "thank you," "hello," and "good-bye," will make you popular. Learning about and respecting the different customs will also help you meet people.	Just because people are dressed differently or look "exotic" does not mean they will appreciate being in your photo album. If you want to take someone's picture, take the time to ask for permission first.

Task 31

Look at these pictures that show different events from the same trip. Imagine that these things happened to you.

First tell your partner about your trip. Then find out about your partner's trip.

> It was an interesting vacation because I . . .

Task 32

Here are some more detailed clues about John.

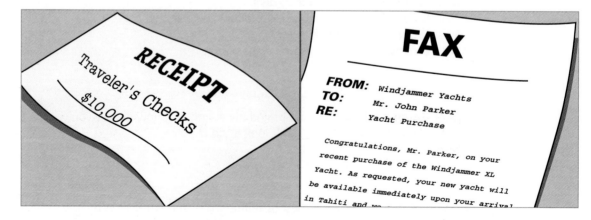

RECEIPT
Traveler's Checks
$10,000

FAX

FROM: Windjammer Yachts
TO: Mr. John Parker
RE: Yacht Purchase

Congratulations, Mr. Parker, on your recent purchase of the Windjammer XL Yacht. As requested, your new yacht will be available immediately upon your arrival in Tahiti and we

Task 33   Your partner is going to call you. Sit back-to-back so that you use only your voices to communicate. Your partner will ask to speak to two people. They are not available. Take the messages.

Message 1

Message 2

Now call your partner. Follow the instructions below. Leave messages using your own name.

You want to speak to Max Fielding.

You're calling to give your new telephone number. It's 221-555-1656.

You want him to call you sometime.

You want to speak to Mandy.

You're calling to let her know your flight will be delayed. The new arrival information is Monday the 13th at 3:15 P.M. on Flight CO 776.

Task 34   Read the news story, and then close your book. Try to retell the story in your own words. Do not read the stories aloud to each other.

Marriage of Few Words

A couple in Australia hasn't spoken to each other for 43 years. Doris and Ivan Weeds stopped communicating shortly after their marriage. "We talked nonstop when we were dating," recalled Mrs. Weeds, "and I guess we said everything we had to." The Weeds have lived together in almost total silence, talking happily with friends but saying nothing to each other. About 25 years ago, Mr. Weeds broke his silence to ask his wife if she wanted to go to Thailand for a vacation. She answered, "No." Mrs. Weeds insists that although they do not talk, they love each other very much. "There are many ways to say 'I love you' without actually saying it," she explained.

Task 35   Memorize the main points and the punch line in these funny stories and jokes. Then take turns telling them to your group. Try to make a good impression by telling them in a lively and interesting way.

Man: Doctor, Doctor, I think I need some new glasses!
Waiter: You certainly do, sir. This is a restaurant.

Mrs. Carlson and Mrs. Morton are discussing their daughters.
Mrs. Morton: My daughter is a university student. She's very smart, you know. Every time we get a letter from her, we have to go to the dictionary.
Mrs. Carlson: You're very lucky. Every time we get a letter from our daughter, we have to go to the bank.

Now discuss these questions.
- Who do you think is the best at telling jokes and stories? Why?
- What other funny stories do you know?

Appendix

Activity 2B
page 7

The street signs are:

1. no left turn
2. curve ahead
3. yield ahead
4. deer crossing
5. no crossing
6. railroad crossing
7. traffic light ahead
8. no U-turn
9. two-way traffic
10. kangaroo crossing next 14 kilometers

Activity 3B
page 7

The signs are:

1. No Parking
2. Beware of Dog
3. Staff Only
4. No Running Permitted
5. Watch Out for Pedestrians
6. Keep off the grass

Activity 3B
page 9

The gestures are:

4 I'm thinking.
8 You have a phone call.
2 I'm sorry.
1 I'm puzzled.
9 I'm just kidding.
5 This is a secret.
3 I love you.
6 Calm down.
7 Be quiet.

Activity 2B
page 17

The superstitions are:

1. h
2. c
3. f
4. g
5. a
6. e
7. b
8. d

Activity 2B
page 21

The answers to the vocabulary definitions are:

1. f
2. c
3. g
4. h
5. b
6. d
7. e
8. a

Activity 2B

page 23

Add up your score for the quiz on page 23 before you read this.

Score	Evaluation
0–6	You don't seem to manage your time very well. Try to use some of the ideas in the quiz to help you study more effectively, and remember that no one concentrates on studying all the time.
7–12	Some of the things you do to help you study are fine and helpful, but maybe you should think again about some of the ideas in the quiz. They may help you to become an even more effective learner.
13–18	You are very well organized. You apply yourself to your studies intelligently and try to make the most of your time. Take another look at some of the things in the quiz you rarely or never do. They could be helpful.
19–24	You seem to be the perfect student. You will undoubtedly do well in your studies.

Activity 2B

page 25

Here is the correct information about the people.

Marilyn Monroe did not star in *Breakfast at Tiffany's*.
Bruce Lee was Chinese-American.
James Dean was not a rock 'n' roll singer.
Vincent van Gogh was a Dutch artist.
Princess Diana died in 1997.

Activity 1C

page 28

Here are the answers to the languages quiz, plus how to say "thank you" in each language.

1. c Thank you.
2. h Khob khun khrab.
3. a Spasibo.
4. e Gracias.
5. i Danke schön.

6. j Arigatō gozaimasu.
7. f Xìe xìe.
8. b Obrigado.
9. d Shokran.
10. g Kamsahamnida.

Activity 3B

page 29

The answers to the quiz are:

1. The capitals and countries are:
   Madrid, Spain
   Lima, Peru
   Cairo, Egypt
   Kuala Lumpur, Malaysia
   Caracas, Venezuela
   Moscow, Russia

2. In order of population:
   1 China
   2 the United States
   3 Indonesia
   4 Japan
   5 Germany
   6 Canada

3. In order from left to right: Canada, Japan, Mexico, Brazil, Thailand, Australia

4. largest country = Russia
   longest river = the Nile

   smallest country = Vatican City
   highest mountain = Mount Everest

Activity 2D

page 35

The interpretation of your quiz score is:

Score	Interpretation
0–13	You're so multiskilled, it's unbelievable! Is there anything you can't do?
14–26	You can do many things. Be careful that other people don't take advantage of you and get you to do everything for them.
27–39	You're a talented person who can do most of the things you need to do.
40–52	Although you're good at doing some things, maybe you could learn to do some more things that you find difficult.
45–64	It's important that you learn to do some things yourself. Until then, don't live alone.

Activity 1B

page 38

Here's some information about the treatments.

Acupuncture – a treatment for pain and illness in which thin needles are positioned just under the surface of the skin

Aromatherapy – a form of treatment in which pleasant-smelling oils are rubbed into the skin, or the scent that they produce is inhaled

Chiropractic adjustment – a treatment involving the manipulation of the spinal column

Massage – pressing or rubbing someone's body with regular, repeated motions in order to relax the person or to reduce pain in joints or muscles

Herbal medicine – treatments that utilize the healing effects of natural herbs and plants rather than modern synthetic drugs

Reflexology – a treatment in which the bottom part of the foot is rubbed gently in order to improve blood flow and to help the person relax

Activity 1B

page 40

The answers to the quiz about life experiences that cause stress are:
1. having an illness or injury
2. getting married
3. being fired from work
4. retiring from work
5. having trouble with in-laws
6. starting or finishing school
7. having trouble with your boss
8. going on vacation

Activity 3C

page 45

The answers to the volcano quiz are:
1. a
2. none have volcanoes
3. all have active volcanoes
4. c
5. c

Activity 1C

page 46

The stories that followed the newspaper headlines on page 46 are:

"Titanic" fan travels the world to break all records

Anna Garcia's favorite movie is *Titanic*. She has seen it 1,000 times since it was first released – in 1,000 different theaters. She has traveled all over the world to see the movie, each time in a different theater. Although, according to the *Guinness Book of World Records*, other people have seen a movie more than 1,000 times, previous record holders have seen it in the same theater. Garcia intends to continue seeing the movie in theaters. "It's just not the same on video," she says.

Robber's ID Badge Leads to Arrest

A bank robber who held up a bank last week in Sydney, Australia, was wearing a ski mask so he would not be recognized. What he forgot to do was remove the security badge he was wearing from his evening job at a fast-food restaurant. The badge had his full name on it. After the robbery, the bank staff notified the police, who looked him up in the phone book, drove to his home, and arrested him.

Activity 1A

page 48

The answers to the definitions are:

1. d	6. f
2. g	7. j
3. b	8. e
4. c	9. i
5. a	10. h

Activity 1C

page 58

Add up your scores for the test. Then check the interpretation.

	Never	Sometimes	Usually	Always
1.	3	2	1	0
2.	0	1	2	3
3.	3	2	1	0
4.	3	2	1	0
5.	0	1	2	3
6.	3	2	1	0
7.	0	1	2	3
8.	3	2	1	0
9.	3	2	1	0
10.	3	2	1	0

Score	Interpretation
0–7	You always try to avoid danger and never take risks. Maybe you're too careful!
8–15	You prefer to "play it safe," and you avoid taking too many risks. You're a pretty careful person.
16–23	You do take risks and don't worry about putting yourself in danger. Perhaps you should be more careful.
24–30	You like to live dangerously. You get a real thrill out of taking risks.

The interpretation of your quiz score is:

Score	Evaluation
36–45	You are a fantastic conversationalist – the life and soul of the party! People love to have you in their group.
27–35	You're a good conversationalist. People enjoy talking to you, and you like talking to them. You're both a good talker and a good listener.
18–26	You could probably do more to improve your conversational skills. Maybe take care to listen to what others are saying before interrupting them.
9–17	You are perhaps a good listener, but you don't say much in conversations. When you do speak, you sometimes try to dominate the conversation.

The model notes of the two phone messages from are:

①
Sharon called to see if Tuesday's dinner is still on
can't get there till 8
call her at work tomorrow

②
Sam Lee from Delta Systems called
has questions about order
call him ASAP: 714-555-0362

The answers to the puzzle are:

201	202	203	204
Alberto	Brian	Craig	David

101	102	103	104
Etsuko	Fran	Gina	Hannah

Self-study

Dear student,

The following section is for use with the Self-study CD. These listening activities will give you an opportunity to improve your listening comprehension at home. The listening sections you'll hear on the CD come directly from the 16 units in *Let's Talk 3* Student's Book. You can use these pages on your own if you have difficulty with an activity in class or just want additional listening practice.

When you see ✳ in a lesson, you know that you can also hear the same listening on the Self-study CD. Usually the whole passage is on the CD, but sometimes only part is included.

Important: Do not listen to the Self-study CD for a lesson until after you study the lesson in class. However, after the lesson you may listen as many times as you'd like. You can check your answers beginning on page 108.

A separate grammar reference section is also included. Look at this section if you have particular grammar questions or problems.

Self-study

A Listen to the four conversations. Check (✔) the expressions you hear.

1. ☑ I'm sorry I'm late.
   ☐ Sorry to be late.

2. ☐ I haven't seen you for a while.
   ☐ I haven't seen you for a long time.

3. ☐ It's nice to meet you.
   ☐ It's nice to see you again.

4. ☐ Give me a kiss.
   ☐ Give me a hug.

B Listen to the four conversations again. Fill in the missing words.

1. Mr. Brown: Thank you for agreeing to meet with me this morning.

   Mr. Lopez: ....*No*........ .....*problem*...... . I've heard a lot of good things
   about you from the accounting department, and...well, I was
   looking forward to getting a chance to meet you in person . . .

2. Maria: Fine, fine. I have a full schedule this semester, so I'm really busy.

   Jenny: Yeah, yeah, me, too. ....
   ....
   and, ah, you know, have lunch or something.

3. Mr. Lee: Ah, nice meeting you, too. ....
   ....
   .... ?

   Mr. Tanaka: Yes, I am. It's a very beautiful city. And...uh...the subway system
   is really . . .

4. Mary: I brought back some great pictures, but . . .

   Susan: ....
   ....

A Listen to the four announcements. Write the number of the announcement next to its purpose.

.... to tell passengers that their plane will leave from a different location
...1... to tell passengers to hurry because their flight is going to leave
.... to tell people that a flight is going to take off late
.... to tell people who need extra help to board the plane

B Listen to announcements 1 and 2 again. Correct the two mistakes in each announcement.

Announcement 1

112
Last call for any remaining passengers on All Nippon Airways Flight ~~120~~ to Osaka. This is the last and final call for this flight. Passengers are requested to proceed immediately to Gate 222.

Announcement 2

At this time, we are now ready to stop boarding China Airlines Flight 666. Passengers requiring special meals are asked to please proceed now to Gate 28 for priority boarding.

C Read announcements 3 and 4. Fill in the blanks with the best words from the box. Then listen and check your answers.

gate	delayed	depart	incoming	arrival	passengers

Announcement 3

Your attention, please. Singapore Airlines Flight 118 to Kuala Lumpur has been .....*delayed*..... due to the late .... of the .... aircraft. This
.........1.................................2...........................3
flight is now scheduled to depart at 9:55.

Announcement 4

Your attention, please. There's been a .... change for ....
...............................1..2
on Philippine Airlines Flight 504 to Manila. This flight will now ....
....3
from Gate 35.

A Listen to the radio show, and answer the questions.

1. How many Sherlock Holmes short stories are there? ...56...............
2. About how many novels did Agatha Christie write? ....
3. How many novels feature Inspector Maigret? ....
4. How many novels feature Philip Marlowe? ....

B Listen to these parts from the radio show again. Correct the two mistakes in each part.

Sherlock Holmes

Well, the first really popular character in detective fiction was the Englishman Sherlock Holmes, who first appeared in a story in 1887. His creator, Sir Arthur Conan Doyle, was a medical doctor. Holmes's exploits were narrated by Dr. Watson and were continued in four novels and 56 short stories. Doyle's most famous novel was *The Hound of the Baskervilles*, published in 1902. In this great story, a man is found dead in a ~~lovely~~ *lonely* area, and everyone believes he has been eaten by a big, ferocious dog. Sherlock Holmes arrives to investigate and finds out whether the dog really exists. *fierce*

Miss Marple

Her books have been translated into every major language. One of her most famous creations was the Englishwoman Miss Marple. Agatha Christie wrote nearly a hundred novels, including the famous Miss Marple mystery *4:50 from Paddington*. In this wonderful story, Miss Marple's mother sees a woman being strangled on a train that is passing by. Miss Marple investigates the mystery by becoming a detective employed by the suspects.

Inspector Maigret

Simenon is best known for his detective novels featuring French Police Inspector Maigret. He's the hero of more than 75 novels, including my all-time favorite, *The Man on the Eiffel Tower*. In this story, a body is found under the famous Eiffel Tower in Paris, and Inspector Maigret solves the murder by finding out about the criminal's motives and biography.

Philip Marlowe

Although he appeared in only seven novels, Philip Marlowe is the typical American detective: tough and incorruptible in his dealings with criminals. Marlowe narrates each story, so we see the world through his eyes. Six of his stories have been made into movies, including *The Big Sleep*, filmed in 1946, with Humphrey Bogart as Marlowe. In this story, Marlowe is employed to investigate a general's daughter and ends up falling in love with that daughter's younger sister.

A Listen to story 1. Fill in the missing words and expressions.

Sure.	OK.	Right.	Huh.
Oh, no!	Yeah?	Oh, yeah.	

Man: Do you want to hear an interesting story?

Woman: .....*Oh, yeah.*.....
    1

Man: I...I heard this really happened.

Woman: ....
    2

Man: There was this eight-year-old boy who dreamed of going to Brazil. Well, after school one day, he went to the airport, you know, on the subway, and...um...he looked around for a family with...lots of luggage and lots of children.

Woman: ....
    3

Man: He even thought to take his passport with him.

Woman: ....
    4

Man: So, he followed the family through passport control, and then he just waited in the departure lounge.

Woman: Right.

Man: Now, when he saw the family get up, . . .

Woman: ....
    5

Man: . . . he followed them and got on the plane.

Woman: ....
    6

Man: The cabin crew thought that there was a mix-up, so they let him on and they found him a seat.

Woman: ....
    7

Man: This kid ended up going all the way to Rio de Janeiro.

Woman: Oh, no!

B Listen to story 2. Number the events in order from 1 to 8.

.... An older couple asked him inside.
.... The dog followed him into the house.
.... Outside one house, he saw a big dog.
...1... A young man was introducing himself to his neighbors.
.... The dog ate a cookie and climbed onto the man's lap.
.... The woman reminded him to take his dog.
.... He rang the doorbell.
.... He thanked the couple and left.

A Listen to Amy's story. Mark the statements True (**T**) or False (**F**).

1. ...*F*... Amy didn't want to change from private school to public school.
√ 2. .... All of her friends attended public school.
3. .... Amy wasn't afraid of starting at a public school.
4. .... Her new high school was fairly small.
5. .... She bought fashionable clothes to wear to her school.
√ 6. .... The classes at her new school had a lot of students.
√ 7. .... She missed the structure of her junior high school.

B Listen to Patrick's story, and answer the questions.

1. What did Patrick wear on his first day of school?
   ...*a tie*..

2. How did he feel that day?
   ....

3. Who took him to school?
   ....

4. What was his teacher like?
   ....

5. What did the kids in his neighborhood do together?
   ....

6. How did Patrick feel about his high school days?
   ....

C Listen to Karen's story. Check (✔) the things she says about her first day of school.

1. ✔ She was happy about starting at her new school.
2. ☐ Most of her friends were starting at another high school.
3. ☐ She didn't know anyone in her first-period class.
4. ☐ She loved high school.
5. ☐ Her grades were terrible.
6. ☐ The schoolwork was too easy for her.
7. ☐ She liked junior high school better than high school.

A Listen to the descriptions of two people. Write **SB** by the details about the Sultan of Brunei and **BG** by the details about Bill Gates.

1. ..*SB*.. has four sons
2. .... built a theme park
3. .... is the world's richest man
4. .... has seven pavilions in his home
5. .... plays polo
6. .... plays golf
7. .... loves to read books
8. .... enjoys flying helicopters

B Listen again to the description of the Sultan of Brunei. Fill in the missing numbers and dates.

The ruler of Brunei, a tiny country in Southeast Asia, is one of the world's richest people. He…he was born in ....*1946*........ , and took over from his father in ....$_2$........ , becoming the ....$_3$........ Sultan of Brunei. He holds the title of Prime Minister as…as well as Sultan. His current total wealth is ....$_4$........ dollars, which comes from the rich resources of oil and gas. Uh…He's married, with four sons and six daughters.

His incredible palace cost 450 million dollars to build and contains 1,778 rooms. Uh…He's very generous to his ....$_5$........ people, most of whom are government employees. Once, he even celebrated his birthday by giving his people a free concert by Michael Jackson. Uh…He…he's also built a fantastic theme park where all the rides are free. Oh, and…and in his spare time, he plays polo as well as squash and badminton. He also enjoys flying helicopters.

C Listen again to the description of Bill Gates, and answer the questions.

1. How old was Bill when he started Microsoft? ..*19*.........................
2. Who is Melinda French? ....
3. What is special about the artwork on the walls of his house? ....
4. What does the central computer do for visitors? ....
5. What do guests select from a computer console? ....
6. What does the sound do? ....

A Listen to Norman's story. Mark the statements True (**T**) or False (**F**).

1. ...T... Norman is from Toronto.
2. .... Two years ago he visited Spain.
3. .... He flew directly to Naples.
4. .... Naples was much more dangerous than Toronto.
5. .... The people in Naples were friendly.
6. .... A woman stole his map.
7. .... She scolded him in English.

B Listen to Lucinda's story. Correct the six mistakes.

I'm from Detroit, Michigan, in the United States, and...uh...my ~~junior~~ *senior* year in high school I won a scholarship to study singing for the summer in London, Ontario. So, I went there and I was actually able to stay in someone's private home, so I really got the inside view, you know, of what it's like to live there, and I loved it. But I have to say, one thing that really surprised me was that you had to go to so many different stores to do your shopping. You know, in Detroit, you just go to one grocery store and everything's there, but in London, there was, like, the bakery, then there was, like, the fish store, and then there was your fruits and vegetables in another store, and that...that really surprised me. But, uh, the people were...were very silent, and it was a really fun summer. But I did – I was also surprised by how many similarities there are in the language! I figured English was English, but they said things like "lift" for "elevator," and "ring you on" instead of "give you a call," and that kind of stuff. It took me a little while to figure it all out, but it was fun.

C Listen to Sung-Jae's story about Hong Kong. Check (✔) the exact adjectives he uses to describe the city.

- ✔ huge
- ☐ enormous
- ☐ interesting
- ☐ crazy
- ☐ crowded
- ☐ incredible
- ☐ intimidating
- ☐ strange
- ☐ unique
- ☐ amazing
- ☐ big
- ☐ noisy

Unit 8

A Listen to Daniel talking about his remote controls. Write the electronic devices they are used for.

1. ...TV...
2. ....
3. ....
4. ....
5. ....
6. ....

B Listen to Rosa's problem. Number the events in order from 1 to 7.

.... If she pressed "2," she could have another option.
.... She got disconnected.
.... She heard a recorded message.
...1... She had a complaint and called customer service.
.... If she pressed "1," she could have one option.
.... She didn't want options; she wanted to talk to a person.
.... She was switched over to a person.

C Listen to Bob's problem. Number the events in order from 1 to 8.

.... The paper started tearing on the book.
...1... He bought a book for a friend.
.... The back of the book was covered with sticky stuff.
.... He tried to take the sticker off the back of the book.
.... He started peeling away at the corner.
.... He tried to rub it off, and it turned black.
.... He tried to get it off from the other side.
.... He got the sticker off.

D Listen to Susan talking about her cell phone. Fill in the missing words.

Well,…uh…I got this nifty new cell phone, and let me tell you, I love cell phones. I love being able to walk down the street and call anybody. But I got this cell phone with voice-activated dialing, so all you have to do is say, "...Call home...," and it dials it for you. Or, "........................," and it dials the number for you. So…uh…last week I was walking down the street and I said, "Call home," and it called .... And then I said, "Call Larry," and it called .... So I've stopped using voice-activated dialing.

E Listen to Frederick talking about his cash card. Mark the statements True (**T**) or False (**F**).

1. ...T... Frederick wanted to get money from a bank machine.
2. .... He typed his PIN number only twice.
3. .... The machine was broken.
4. .... The machine "ate" his bank card.
5. .... Frederick had put the wrong card in the machine.

A Listen to Jared's story. Fill in the missing words.

You see, I come from a small town. When I started going to ......*college*...... in a
1
large city, I felt really .... and…and .... I didn't know
2   3
anybody. I didn't know what to do with myself on the weekends. It was hard to
make friends, but…then, someone told me about the .... club. I went
4
over there and ...., and…I got in. Now I have a lot of new friends
5
there, and I'm busy every weekend with .... and performances.
6
It's great!

B Listen to Maria's story. Correct the three mistakes.

             medical
Well, I'm in ~~art~~ school now. But when I was preparing for the entrance exam, I
was so stressed out. There was so much material that I had to copy! I was so
scared I wouldn't be able to pass that test that I started to panic. Well, I learned to
organize my time much better, and I started a drama group with some of my
friends. Well, of course, in the end I passed the exam, and so did they!

C Listen to John's story. Correct the three mistakes.

I work at an Internet company. Um…We're a new company, so…you know, it
                                work
always seems like there's more ~~money~~ than we can possibly handle. Sometimes we
work really short hours – easily until after nine or ten at night. Well, I really
needed to do something crazy after work to…uh…to relieve stress. So I started
taking ballroom dancing lessons. It…it's incredibly fun,…and I've gotten pretty
good at it. I even enter ballroom dancing competitions!

D Listen to Emi's story, and answer the questions.

1. What was Emi's job at the large company? *administrative assistant*
2. How was the pay there? ....
3. How did she feel about that job? ....
4. What did she suddenly do one day? ....
5. What kind of job does she have now? ....
6. How does she feel about it? ....

E Listen to Doug's story. Write four things he does on the train.

1.   *relaxes* ....
2. ....
3. ....
4. ....

A Read this part of the lecture about volcanoes. Fill in the blanks with the best words from the box. Then listen and check your answers.

cool	dormant	magma	extinct	active	melts	volcanic

Lecturer: OK, everyone, let's get started. Um…Today I'm going to…focus on some of the benefits of ….._volcanic_..... activity. A volcano doesn't always bring disaster. First, let's take a look at how volcanoes work. They are a natural way that the Earth and other planets ....2................. off. A planet is warm inside, and the heat sometimes escapes towards its surface. This heat sometimes ....3................. rock, which then rises towards the planet's surface. When the hot rock, called ....4................. , breaks through the crust, an eruption occurs….Yes?

Student: Um…What's the difference between an active volcano and an extinct volcano?

Lecturer: Ah! An ....5................. volcano is one that has erupted recently or may erupt at any time. The world is full of ....6................. volcanoes – these are ones that haven't erupted for hundreds or thousands of years but may erupt again. The eruption of Mount Pinatubo in the Philippines in 1991 was the largest eruption of the twentieth century – its first eruption in 600 years. An ....7................. volcano is one that has stopped erupting altogether. OK?

B Listen to the last part of the lecture. Correct the six mistakes.

So, what about the ~~disasters~~? _benefits_ Well, one of the most pleasurable things to do in an area where there are volcanoes is to visit hot drinks. It's very relaxing to take a bath in the hot, mineral-filled water, and many people believe it's good for you, too. Also, volcanoes can save money by providing hot water for heating. In countries such as Iceland, water that's heated by volcanic activity can be used to generate electricity. Another bad thing about volcanoes is that their lava and volcanic ash contain minerals that make soil fertile. You know, the beautiful green area around Italy's Mount Vesuvius is a good example of this. And finally, volcanoes are often good for business. Local people can set up businesses, taking tourists to see the volcanic landscapes. Geysers like those in New Zealand, or Old Faithful in Yellowstone Park, are very popular tourist attractions. Um…These are just a few of the ways we can use the lava of volcanoes to improve our lives.

A Listen to Alan's story. Number the events in order from 1 to 8.

.... The train had stopped.

.... The kids started laughing.

...1... Going around the curve, he saw a yellow bus.

.... He stepped on the brakes.

.... He opened his eyes.

.... He and the bus driver hugged each other.

.... The kids got out of the bus.

.... He shut his eyes.

B Listen to Betty's story. Correct the five mistakes.

OK. I was taking the kids home after ~~work~~ *school* when this white truck ahead of us suddenly stopped just on the other side of the railroad tracks. I couldn't back up because there was another bus and a long line of cars behind me. There was nothing I could do. I felt there might be a train coming along any minute. I immediately stood up and…and told all the kids to get off the bus and run away from the tracks. But I stayed on the bus after all the kids had gotten off, in case the truck ahead moved and I could drive off the tracks. Well, the driver of the car behind me got out and took off his bright blue coat. He ran up the tracks around the curve, waving the coat. He was the hero. The train engineer saw him before the curve and hit the brakes. As it came around the curve, I could see the train braking. I…I just sat in my seat waiting for the truck to hit the bus – th - there was no way it could stop, I thought. But it did! Afterwards, everyone gathered around, hugging each other. Talk about lucky!

C Listen to Crystal's story. Mark the statements True (**T**) or False (**F**).

1. ...F... Crystal was on the bus.
2. .... Ahead of the bus was a new blue car.
3. .... The school bus couldn't back up.
4. .... The man in the car behind the bus jumped out.
5. .... He was wearing a blue T-shirt.
6. .... The train came around the curve slowly.
7. .... The train hit the bus.

A Listen to Donna talking about her best friend, and answer the questions.

1. What is Donna's best friend's name? ...*Alisa*...............................
2. In what city did they meet? ....
3. Where did Donna go on a trip? ....
4. How long did her friend stay with her? ....
5. How was their vacation? ....

B Listen to Greg talking about his best friend. Fill in the missing words.

Uh…My best friend would be my friend Elizabeth. We've been friends for a long time. We met…um…the very first day of ......*college*......, and we became friends in about five minutes. And I guess what I like best about her is, no matter when we get together or how much time we spend together, we .... never run out of things to say. We can talk to each other .... It sort of .... her parents – she lives in…in Miami now. And we talk on the phone, and they look at the phone bills and say: "You talked for two hours on Monday – how can you talk for two hours again on Tuesday? .... could have happened in between." But, ... nothing has to, we just get together and laugh. We…uh…we once got together and we had to make up a big .... of things that we did, because all we did was sit around together and talk .... and laugh. We never went to a movie or a play. We'd just go to restaurants and spend time together and laugh.

C Listen to Sophia talking about her best friend. Mark the statements True (**T**) or False (**F**).

1. ...*F*... Sophie's best friend's name is Greg.
2. .... She studied singing at college.
3. .... Her friend is a guitar player.
4. .... He has a great sense of humor.
5. .... They like to perform plays together.
6. .... He's a very good talker.

A Listen to Jane's frightening experience. Number the events in order from 1 to 6.

.... She looked down and saw a snake moving away.

.... One dark night, she came out of the cabin wearing sandals.

.... She screamed and ran back to her cabin.

...1... She decided to become a camp counselor.

.... She heard something rustle.

.... Something moved over her foot.

B Listen to Tony's frightening experience. Correct the five mistakes.

frightening

I had a ~~funny~~ thing happen when I was in Buffalo. Um…We had rented a car and we were driving to Niagara, and…we…uh…we sort of got lost, but we didn't much care because we had some food and we knew if we followed road signs, we'd find our way eventually. But then this fog settled in, and we couldn't see *anything*. And we began to get scared that if we went anywhere, we'd be taking ourselves further and further out of our way, and that we might never find our way to Niagara. So…we…uh…we started crawling down the road – you couldn't tell where the edge of the road was, that was another frightening thing. You didn't know if you were on the road or off. So after a little while, we finally see this set of…uh…headlights in front of us, and we just thought: "Well, maybe they're local, we'll follow them." And we followed them and followed them and figured wherever they go, we'll go. And finally, they came to a complete stop, and they didn't seem to be moving. So I got out of my car and I yelled: "Do you want to tell me why you've just come to a dead stop?" And the driver of the other car said: "Do you want to tell me what you're doing in my garden?"

C Listen to Mary's frightening experience, and answer the questions.

1. Where does Mary live? ....

2. What happened one day on her way to work? ....

3. What was it like inside the train? ....

4. How did the passengers feel? ....

5. What happened when they got to the next station? ....

A Listen to Tom's answer. Mark the statements True (**T**) or False (**F**).

1. ...T... He's finishing his undergraduate degree.
2. .... He wants to go to law school.
3. .... He wants to go to school in Washington.
4. .... He wants to help wealthy people.
5. .... He hopes that being a lawyer will help him become a doctor.
6. .... He wants a larger office.

B Listen to Young-Joon and Marianne's answers. Fill in the missing words.

Young-Joon: Well, one thing I've always wanted to ..*accomplish*.. in my life is
to travel a lot, and...I'd like to .... it with my love of
kind of the sports and what-not. And one thing I'd love to do is to
.... all up and down...uh...the Atlantic coast, starting in
Maine and sailing all the way down, and maybe even continue down
into South America. I think that would just be a wonderful
.... – to have a sailboat, and out on the sea, and just
going from island to island. That...that was ....
something I'd like to do.

Interviewer: Good. Thank you. And, finally, Marianne. You've heard the others.
Tell us what you'd like to accomplish in your life.

Marianne: Well, actually, ...um...tomorrow I .... from a three-month
course that I took called Training for Trades.

Interviewer: Mm-hmm.

Marianne: And it's to get more women and minority men, actually, into the
trades – into the carpentry, electrical, masonry. And what I'd like
to do with this is start a .... company run by women,
myself being one of them. And I would like to get work...uh...
.... Victorian homes.

A Listen to what Rachel says in conversation 1. Mark the statements True (**T**) or False (**F**).

1. ...T... Yesterday, there were fifteen people on the tour.
2. .... The walk up the mountain is very difficult.
3. .... They will try to get up the mountain by sunrise.
4. .... After they climb the mountain, they will have breakfast.
5. .... She says they will need sunglasses.
6. .... Lunch will be chicken and salad.
7. .... They will go snorkeling in the afternoon.
8. .... They need to buy masks and snorkels.
9. .... They will go shopping later.

B Read this part of conversation 2. Try to guess the missing words. Then listen and check your answers.

> Woman 2: Excuse me, what kinds of things are we going to do?
>
> Jack: Well, in the morning we drive around the south of the island. Our first stop is Pigeon Point, where there is a beautiful view of the water below. And...and then we visit a small ice-cream .....*factory*....., where you can see our delicious island ice cream being made.
>
> Man: What flavors are there?
>
> Jack: Ah...coconut, mango, papaya, and .... , I think.
>
> Man: Do we get free samples?
>
> Jack: Oh,...you bet! We...we then continue around the island, enjoying beautiful views of the Atlantic coast. And we stop for lunch at a nice .... cafe. After lunch, we head north, stopping at a beach, like I said earlier, and finally we go to the nature reserve, where you can see parrots and ....
>
> Everyone: Ahhh! Fun!
>
> Woman 1: Um...So, what's for lunch?
>
> Jack: Uh...For lunch? A typical .... lunch.
>
> Woman 1: What's that?
>
> Jack: Spicy chicken, rice and beans, and .... tropical fruit for dessert.
>
> Everyone: Mmmm.
>
> Jack: You get a fresh lime drink, but if you want any other drinks, that costs extra.
>
> Woman 1: Oh,...uh...Jack, excuse me, but are there any other extra costs?
>
> Jack: Well, you might want to buy some .... , like local crafts or jewelry. And you might want to tip your driver. Any more questions?

A Listen to Dr. Alexander's lecture. Mark the statements True (**T**) or False (**F**) or Not Sure (**?**).

1. ...*F*... Dr. Alexander's lecture is on the visible differences between men and women.
2. .... The size and form of men's and women's brains is very different.
3. .... Some scientists now believe that men's and women's brains are different.
4. .... Men's and women's brains are different at birth.
5. .... Women tend to do better at language tasks.
6. .... Men tend to be better at mathematics.
7. .... Two men and two women took part in the experiment.
8. .... In the second task, letters were symbols without meaning.

B Listen to this part of Dr. Alexander's lecture again. Correct the seven mistakes.

Now, maybe some of this will be clearer if we take a look at a ~~modern~~ *recent* experiment. In this experiment, ten men and ten women were given two difficult tasks. The first task involved handling words and concepts: The volunteers were faced with words like…uh…like "lion" and "chair," and asked to place them in categories of "alive" or "lifeless." The second task involved recognizing meanings: The volunteers were shown letters from the alphabet, and then they were asked to press a button when a particular sequence came up. Now, the men did better on the first task, where the words were associated with their meanings. The scientists did better, on the other hand, on the second task, where the letters were…uh…they were just symbols without meaning. I tell you what…I tell you what. Let's…let's try a little experiment on our own, OK? All the men should form one group, and all the women should form another group. Then, I want you to take out a piece of paper. Then, I'll take a look at the results of the questionnaire, and we'll go from there and figure out . . .

Self-study answer key

Unit 1

A

1. I'm sorry I'm late.
2. I haven't seen you for a while.
3. It's nice to meet you.
4. Give me a hug.

B

1. No problem.
2. We should try to get together sometime.
3. Are you enjoying your visit to our city?
4. I can't wait to see them.

Unit 2

A

4 to tell passengers that their plane will leave from a different location
1 to tell passengers to hurry because their flight is going to leave
3 to tell people that a flight is going to take off late
2 to tell people who need extra help to board the plane

B

Announcement 1
1. Flight ~~120~~   Flight 112
2. Gate ~~222~~   Gate 22

Announcement 2
1. ready to ~~stop~~   ready to begin
2. requiring special ~~meals~~   requiring special assistance

C

Announcement 3	**Announcement 4**
1. delayed	1. gate
2. arrival	2. passengers
3. incoming	3. depart

Unit 3

A

1. 56   2. about 100   3. more than 75   4. 7

B

Sherlock Holmes
1. a ~~lovely~~ area   a lonely area
2. has been ~~eaten~~   has been killed

Miss Marple
1. Miss Marple's ~~mother~~   Miss Marple's friend
2. becoming a ~~detective~~   becoming a servant

Inspector Maigret
1. a body is found ~~under~~   a body is found on
2. motives and ~~biography~~   motives and psychology

Philip Marlowe
1. employed to ~~investigate~~   employed to protect
2. daughter's ~~younger~~ sister   daughter's older sister

Unit 4

A

1. Oh, yeah.   4. Huh.   6. Oh, no!
2. OK.   5. Yeah?   7. Sure.
3. Right.

B

4 An older couple asked him inside.
5 The dog followed him into the house.
2 Outside one house, he saw a big dog.
1 A young man was introducing himself to his neighbors.
6 The dog ate a cookie and climbed onto the man's lap.
8 The woman reminded him to take his dog.
3 He rang the doorbell.
7 He thanked the couple and left.

Unit 5

A

1. F   5. F
2. T   6. T
3. F   7. T
4. F

B

1. a tie   4. warm
2. scared and excited   5. study
3. his dad   6. It was fun./It was a good experience.

C

2. Most of her friends were starting at another high school.
6. The schoolwork was too easy for her.
7. She liked junior high school better than high school.

Unit 6

A

1. SB   5. SB
2. SB   6. BG
3. BG   7. BG
4. BG   8. SB

B

1. 1946   4. 30 billion
2. 1967   5. 300,000
3. 29th

C

1. 19
2. his wife/a Microsoft employee
3. It can be changed
   (to suit the occupier's mood).
4. It opens doors and turns lights on and off.
5. music
6. follows them

Unit 7 **A**

1. T   4. F   6. F
2. F   5. T   7. F
3. F

B

1. my ~~junior~~ year   my senior year
2. London, ~~Ontario~~   London, England
3. the ~~fish~~ store   the meat store
4. how many ~~similarities~~   how many differences
5. were very ~~silent~~   were very sweet
6. "ring you ~~on~~"   "ring you up"

C

huge
crazy
intimidating
unique
amazing
big

Unit 8 **A**

1. TV   3. cable   5. CD player
2. VCR   4. stereo   6. air conditioner

B

4 If she pressed "2," she could have another option.
7 She got disconnected.
2 She heard a recorded message.
1 She had a complaint and called customer service.
3 If she pressed "1," she could have one option.
5 She didn't want options; she wanted to talk to a person.
6 She was switched over to a person.

C

4 The paper started tearing on the book.
1 He bought a book for a friend.
7 The back of the book was covered with sticky stuff.
2 He tried to take the sticker off the back of the book.
3 He started peeling away at the corner.
8 He tried to rub it off, and it turned black.
5 He tried to get it off from the other side.
6 He got the sticker off.

D

1. Call home
2. Call Larry
3. my mom
4. Harry

E

1. T
2. F
3. F
4. T
5. T

Unit 9

A

1. college
2. confused
3. lonely
4. drama
5. auditioned
6. rehearsals

B

1. I'm in ~~art~~ school   I'm in medical school
2. I had to ~~copy~~   I had to memorize
3. started a ~~drama~~ group   started a study group

C

1. there's more ~~money~~   there's more work
2. really ~~short~~ hours   really long hours
3. something ~~crazy~~ after work something fun after work

D

1. administrative assistant
2. pretty good
3. bored
4. quit
5. works in a flower shop
6. happy

E

1. relaxes
2. drinks coffee
3. reads the paper
4. sleeps

Unit 10

A

1. volcanic
2. cool
3. melts
4. magma
5. active
6. dormant
7. extinct

B

1. what about the ~~disasters~~   what about the benefits
2. to visit hot ~~drinks~~   to visit hot springs
3. can save ~~money~~   can save energy
4. Another ~~bad~~ thing   Another good thing
5. good for ~~business~~   good for tourism
6. we can use the ~~lava~~   we can use the power

A

5 The train had stopped.
7 The kids started laughing.
1 Going around the curve, he saw a yellow bus.
2 He stepped on the brakes.
4 He opened his eyes.
8 He and the bus driver hugged each other.
6 The kids got out of the bus.
3 He shut his eyes.

B

1. home after ~~work~~   home after school
2. there was another ~~bus~~   there was another truck
3. the driver of the ~~car~~   the driver of the truck
4. his bright ~~blue~~ coat   his bright red coat
5. the ~~truck~~ to hit the bus the train to hit the bus

C

1. F	5. F
2. F	6. F
3. T	7. F
4. T	

A

1. Alisa	4. a week
2. New York City	5. great
3. Los Angeles	

B

1. college	5. Nothing
2. absolutely	6. apparently
3. nonstop	7. itinerary
4. amazes	8. constantly

C

1. F	4. T
2. T	5. F
3. F	6. F

A

5 She looked down and saw a snake moving away.
2 One dark night, she came out of the cabin wearing sandals.
6 She screamed and ran back to her cabin.
1 She decided to become a camp counselor.
3 She heard something rustle.
4 Something moved over her foot.

B

1. I had a ~~funny~~ thing happen   I had a frightening thing happen
2. we had ~~some food~~   we had a map
3. find our way ~~to Niagara~~   find our way home
4. this set of ~~headlights~~   this set of taillights
5. doing in my ~~garden~~   doing in my driveway

C

1. New York City
2. got stuck in the subway
3. dark / hot
4. upset
5. Everybody (on her car) got off.

Unit 14

A

1. T   4. F
2. T   5. F
3. T   6. F

B

1. accomplish   5. definitely
2. combine   6. graduate
3. sail   7. construction
4. adventure   8. remodeling

Unit 15

A

1. T   6. F
2. F   7. T
3. T   8. F
4. T   9. F
5. F

B

1. factory   5. Caribbean
2. banana   6. fresh
3. seaside   7. souvenirs
4. monkeys

Unit 16

A

1. F   4. ?   7. F
2. F   5. T   8. T
3. T   6. T

B

1. a ~~modern~~ experiment   a recent experiment
2. two ~~difficult~~ tasks   two simple tasks
3. like "lion" and "~~chair~~"   like "lion" and "table"
4. involved recognizing ~~meanings~~   involved recognizing patterns
5. Now, the ~~men~~ did better   Now, the women did better
6. The ~~scientists~~ did better   The men did better
7. results of the ~~questionnaire~~   results of the survey

Grammar

REVIEW: VERB TENSES

Simple present tense

Where **do** you **work**?	I **work** at National Bank.
How **do** you **like** your job?	I **don't like** it very much.

Where **does** she **work**?	She **works** at Mike's Cleaners.
How **does** she **like** her job?	She **doesn't like** it very much.

Present continuous tense

What **are** you **doing** these days?	I'm **studying** and **working** part-time.
Where **are** you **going**?	I'm **going** to work. I'm **not going** to the library.

What's he **doing** these days?	He's **traveling** around Europe.
How **is** he **getting** around?	He's **taking** the train. He's **not hitchhiking**.

Simple past tense

What **happened**?	He **had** some problems at work and **left** the country.
Where **did** he **go**?	He probably **went** to Mexico.

Did you **go** out last night?	Yes, I **did**. I **had** a date.
Did you **have** a good time?	No, we **didn't**. We **didn't have** anything in common.

Past continuous tense

What **were** you **doing** when you fell?	I **was going** across the lobby.
Were you **running**?	No, I **wasn't**. I **was walking**.
Was Dan **walking** with you?	Yes, he **was**. He **was carrying** my suitcase.

Present perfect tense

What do you think **has** just **happened**?	I think someone **has** just **left** without paying.
Have you ever **done** anything like that?	No, I **haven't**. I've never **committed** a crime.
Has the manager **called** the police?	Yes, he **has**. They **haven't arrived** yet.

Future with be going to

What **are** you **going to do** this weekend?	I'm **going to go** camping in the mountains.
Are you **going to go** alone?	No, I'm **not**. Two friends **are going to go** with me.
Are they **going to take** a tent?	Yes, they **are**. In fact, they're **going to take** two tents.

Future with will

How **will** the world **be** different in 1000 years?	It **will be** more crowded and more polluted.
Will people **live** on the moon?	Yes, they **will**. They'll **have** small cities there.
Will people **travel** to other planets?	No, they **won't**. Long-distance travel **will be** too expensive.

MODALS AND SIMILAR EXPRESSIONS

Expressing ability: **can, could, be able to**

Can you **speak** Portuguese?	Yes, I **can**. I **can speak** it very well.
Are you **able to speak** Spanish?	No, I'**m** not.
Were you **able to speak** English as a child?	No, I **wasn't**.
Could you **speak** Portuguese?	Yes, I **could**.
Will you **be able to come** to my party tomorrow?	Yes, I **will**, but I **won't be able to stay** long.

Expressing possibility: **may, might, could (= maybe), must (= probably)**

What **could** this sign **mean**?	It **may mean** you can't turn left.
	It **might mean** you can't turn left.
	It **could mean** you can't turn left.
	It **must mean** you can't turn left.
I wonder why they were so late.	They **may have gotten** stuck in traffic.
	They **might have gotten** stuck in traffic.
	They **could have gotten** stuck in traffic.
	They **must have gotten** stuck in traffic.

Expressing impossibility: **can't, couldn't**

There's a call for you. I think it's Teresa.	It **can't be** Teresa. She's on her way to Ireland.
	It **couldn't be** Teresa. She's on her way to Ireland.
Someone called you. I think it was Teresa.	It **couldn't have been** Teresa. She's on her way to Ireland.

Expressing necessity: **have to, must**

We're going to Australia. What **do** we **have to do**?	You **have to get** a passport.
	You **must get** a passport.
	You **don't have to get** a visa.
You went last year. What **did** you **have to do**?	I **had to get** a passport.
	I **didn't have to get** a visa.

Asking for and giving advice: **should, ought to**

What **should** you **do** to have a healthy relationship?	You **should be** generous.
	You **ought to be** generous.
	You **shouldn't play** games.

Saying you made a mistake: **should have**

You stood me up last night!	I'm sorry. I **should have called** you.
	I'm sorry. I **shouldn't have forgotten** our date.

PAST PERFECT TENSE

Wh- questions

How many miles	had	I you he she we they	run before it began to rain?

Affirmative statements

I You He She We They	'd run several miles.

Negative statements

I You He She We They	hadn't been happy until now.

Contractions

'd = had

hadn't = had not

Yes/No questions

Had	I you he she we they	(ever) worked in an office before?

Short answers

Yes, I had. / No, I hadn't.
Yes, you had. / No, you hadn't.
Yes, he had. / No, he hadn't.
Yes, she had. / No, she hadn't.
Yes, we had. / No, we hadn't.
Yes, they had. / No, they hadn't.

PAST PERFECT VS. SIMPLE PAST

Use the simple past to talk about something that happened in the past. Use the past perfect to talk about things that happened before that time.

It was her first day of public high school. She was nervous because she had attended a small private school before.
She hadn't eaten breakfast because she hadn't felt hungry, but now suddenly she needed to eat something.
She found a vending machine, but then she realized she had forgotten to bring money to school with her!

PRESENT AND PAST PERFECT CONTINUOUS

The present perfect continuous emphasizes the duration of an action.

Have you been waiting long?
Yes. I've been standing here for two hours.

The past perfect continuous emphasizes the duration of an action that was in progress before another action or time in the past.

Had you been living in the apartment long before you moved?
Yes. We'd been living there for almost ten years before we finally bought a house.

ACTIVE VOICE VS. PASSIVE VOICE

Use an active verb to say what the subject does.

| The policeman **arrested** Charles. |
| (subject) (object) |

Use a passive verb to say what happens to the subject. In a passive sentence, the object of an active verb becomes the subject of the passive verb.

| Charles **was arrested**. |
| (subject) |

In passive sentences, the person or thing that causes the action is called the agent. If we want to mention the agent, we usually use a phrase with *by*.

| Charles **was arrested** by the policeman. |

Only transitive verbs (verbs followed by an object) can be used in the passive. Intransitive verbs (verbs never followed by an object) cannot be used in the passive.

Active

| Firefighters **put out** the fire. (transitive) |
| The firefighters **arrived** quickly. (intransitive) |

Passive

| The fire **was put out**. |
| ———— |

To form the passive, use *be* + past participle. Here are some examples:

Active	*Passive*
What **do** people **use** this for?	What **is** this **used** for?
The police **are investigating** the crime.	The crime **is being investigated**.
His behavior **surprised** us.	We **were surprised** by his behavior.
It happened while they **were making** the coat.	It happened while the coat **was being made**.
They still **haven't solved** the traffic problems.	The traffic problems still **haven't been solved**.
No one **had invented** the telephone yet.	The telephone **hadn't been invented** yet.
Athletes **will break** many world records this year.	Many world records **will be broken** this year.
They**'re going to build** a new bridge.	A new bridge **is going to be built**.
We **must reduce** air and water pollution.	Air and water pollution **must be reduced**.
Firefighters **should have put out** the fire by now.	The fire **should have been put out** by now.

TAG QUESTIONS

A tag question is made up of a statement followed by a short question, called a tag. The verb in the tag agrees with the verb in the statement.

| A good education is important, **isn't it**? |
| A sense of fashion isn't important, **is it**? |

We usually use tag questions when we want to find out if our information is correct or when we expect the listener to agree. The most common patterns are affirmative sentence + negative tag and negative sentence + affirmative tag.

| You enjoyed the movie, **didn't you**? |
| You didn't have a good time, **did you**? |

| You and Ms. Lee have already met, **haven't you**? |
| You and Bill haven't met yet, **have you**? |

| They should try to compromise, **shouldn't they**? |
| They shouldn't argue anymore, **should they**? |

EMBEDDED QUESTIONS

An embedded question is a question that is included in either another question or a statement. Embedded questions are often used to ask politely for information or to express something that we aren't sure of or don't know.

| Do you know **what time we arrive**? |
| I have no idea **what time it is**. |

We use statement word order – not question word order – in embedded questions. Note that *do, does,* and *did* aren't used in embedded questions.

Direct Wh- question **Embedded question**

| What does this mean? |

Do you have any idea	**what this means**?
Do you know	
I don't know	**what this means**.
I have no idea	

| What's this? |

Can you tell me	**what this is**?
Can you guess	
I'm not sure	**what this is**.
I can't imagine	

If the embedded question is a *yes/no* question, use *if* or *whether*.

Direct Yes/No question **Embedded question**

| Does he like his job? |

Do you know	if	**he likes his job**?
Could you tell us	whether	
I want to know	if	**he likes his job**.
I'm not sure	whether	

| Should I tip the waiter? |

Do you know	if	**I should tip the waiter**?
Can you remember	whether	
I can't remember	if	**I should tip the waiter**.
I'm not sure	whether	

AUXILIARY VERBS IN ADDITIONS AND RESPONSES

Use auxiliary verbs to agree or disagree and to express similarity and contrast.

	Expressing agreement/similarity	*Expressing disagreement/contrast*
I love to travel.	**So do** I/I **do, too**.	You **do**? I **don't**.
We've never been to Mexico.	**Neither have** they./They **haven't either**.	You **haven't**? They **have**.
He's looking for a new car.	**So is** she./She **is, too**.	He **is**? She **isn't**.
She can't program a VCR.	**Neither can** I./I **can't either**.	She **can't**? I **can**.
We saw a great movie last night.	**So did** we./We **did, too**.	You **did**? We **didn't**.
I won't be able to come tomorrow.	**Neither will** I./I **won't either**.	You **won't**? I **will**.

You can also use an auxiliary verb to avoid repeating information.

| Are you ready for your trip? | No, **I'm not**. (= I'm not ready for my trip.) |
| Do you travel much? | I used to, but I **don't** anymore. (= I don't travel much anymore.) |

RELATIVE CLAUSES

A relative clause can describe, identify, or give more information about a noun. Relative pronouns can be used either as the subject of the clause or as the object of the verb.

as the subject of the clause

| A commentator is a person. He or she comments on the news. |
| A commentator is a person **who/that comments on the news.** |

| A safari is an experience. It will teach you a lot. |
| A safari is an experience **which/that will teach you a lot.** |

as the object of the verb

| You need a friend. You can call him or her anytime. |
| You need a friend **(who/whom/that) you can call anytime.** |

| What are some new experiences? You'd like to try them. |
| What are some new experiences **(which/that) you'd like to try?** |

You can omit the relative pronouns as the object of the verb.

| You need a friend **you can call anytime.** |
| What are some new experiences **you'd like to try?** |

Relative clauses often *define* the nouns. These are called defining relative clauses.

defining

| The friend **who/that I told you about** is coming next weekend. |
| I want to move to a city **which/that has a warmer climate.** |

When the relative clause simply *adds* information that is not necessary to identify the noun, set it off by commas. You cannot use *that* in non-defining relative clauses.

non-defining

| My best friend, **who moved to Portland last year,** is a successful lawyer. |
| Portland, **which is a city in the state of Oregon,** receives a lot of rainfall every year. |

Where and *when* can also function as relative pronouns.

| That's the store **where I buy my lottery tickets.** |
| I'll always remember the day **when I met my best friend.** |

REPORTED SPEECH

You can use either direct or reported speech to talk about what someone else said. Note the verb changes.

Direct speech	*Reported speech*
She said, "I **am** opposed to corporal punishment."	She said she **was** opposed to corporal punishment.
He said, "I **don't like** detention."	He said he **didn't like** detention.
He said, "My mother **cried** when Princess Diana died."	He said his mother **had cried** when Princess Diana died.
They said, "We **are going to go** to the beach."	They said they **were going to go** to the beach.
She said, "I **will go** back to school next year."	She said she **would go** back to school the following year.
I said, "I **can pay** you on Tuesday."	I said I **could pay** you on Tuesday.
They said, "We **must get** home by ten."	They said they **had to get** home by ten.

PHRASAL VERBS

A phrasal verb is a verb that changes its meaning when used with a particle. Phrasal verbs are either transitive (they take a direct object) or intransitive (they don't take a direct object).

Transitive

| We have to **pick up** the toys. |

Intransitive

| What time do you have to **get up**? |

Many phrasal verbs can be used either transitively or intransitively.

| I wish he would **give up** smoking. |
| After the police chased him for almost an hour, the thief finally **gave up**. |

Transitive phrasal verbs are either separable or inseparable. With separable phrasal verbs, a noun can come either between the verb and the particle or after the particle.

| You should **write** your study goals **down**. |
| You should **write down** your study goals. |

With separable phrasal verbs, a pronoun *must* come between the verb and the particle.

| You should **write** them **down**. |

With inseparable phrasal verbs, a noun or pronoun must follow the particle.

| I **ran into** Jim yesterday. |
| I **ran into** him yesterday. |

Here are some more examples:

Transitive / Separable	**Transitive / Inseparable**	**Intransitive / Inseparable**
add up	look for	look out
call off	stand by	go out
fill out	take after	hold on

VERBS + INFINITIVE AND/OR GERUND

Some verbs can be followed only by the infinitive or by the gerund form of another verb. Here are some examples.

Verb + infinitive

| She **decided to go** with us. |

agree	fail	manage	promise
appear	hope	mean	refuse
attempt	hurry	offer	seem
choose	intend	plan	want
deserve	learn	pretend	

Verb + gerund

| She **enjoys hiking**. |

admit	deny	keep	resent
advise	dislike	mind	resist
appreciate	finish	miss	risk
avoid	give up	practice	tolerate
can't help	imagine	quit	

Some verbs can be followed by either form with no change in meaning.

Verb + infinitive/gerund: same meaning

| When **did** you **begin to feel/feeling** sick? |
| He **can't stand to get/getting** wet in the rain. |

Some additional verbs

continue	like	prefer
hate	love	start

Some verbs can be followed by either form, but there is a difference in meaning.

Verb + infinitive/gerund: different meaning

| I **remembered to take** my cell phone, and it came in handy. |
| I **remembered taking** my cell phone, so I didn't understand why I couldn't find it. |

Some additional verbs

forget   go on   stop

CONDITIONAL SENTENCES

Possible situations

Use the simple present in the *if* clause and the future in the other clause.

| **If** it **rains** tomorrow, **I'll stay** home and **watch** a video. |
| **If** you**'re not** compatible with your partner, the relationship **won't last.** |

Hypothetical situations

Use the simple past in the *if* clause and *would* + base form of the verb in the other clause.

| **If** someone **asked** me for travel advice, **I'd tell** him or her to buy a rail pass. |
| **If** you **had** the time and money, **would** you **want** to travel? |

Contrary-to-fact situations

Use the past perfect in the *if* clause and *would have* + past participle in the other clause to describe an imaginary situation in the past that is contrary to the actual situation.

| **If** you **had asked** me, I **would have told** you to choose a nonstop flight. |
| **If** I **hadn't had to** change planes, my luggage probably **wouldn't have gotten** lost. |

SENTENCES WITH *WISH*

Use *wish* to say that you want a situation to be different.

Wishes about the present

| I **don't have** any money in the bank. | I **wish** I **had** some money in the bank. |

Wishes about the future

| My friend **won't pay** me **back.** | I **wish** my friend **would pay** me **back.** |

Wishes about the past

| My luggage **got** lost. | I **wish** my luggage **hadn't gotten** lost. |

IRREGULAR VERBS

Verb	Simple past	Past participle	Verb	Simple past	Past participle
be	was/were	been	know	knew	known
break	broke	broken	lose	lost	lost
buy	bought	bought	make	made	made
choose	chose	chosen	meet	met	met
come	came	come	read	read	read
do	did	done	ride	rode	ridden
drink	drank	drunk	say	said	said
drive	drove	driven	see	saw	seen
eat	ate	eaten	sleep	slept	slept
find	found	found	speak	spoke	spoken
fly	flew	flown	spend	spent	spent
give	gave	given	take	took	taken
go	went	gone	think	thought	thought
have	had	had	wear	wore	worn
hear	heard	heard	write	wrote	written

Acknowledgments

Text Credits

39, 77, 83 British Airways, "Exercises for the neck and shoulders," "Exercises for the arms," and "Exercises for the lower back, legs, and feet" from *High Life*. Reprinted with the permission of the publishers.

40 Stressful life changes ranking exercise adapted from T. H. Holmes and R. H. Rahe, "The Social Readjustment Rating Scale" from *Journal of Psychosomatic Research* 11 (1967): 213–218. Copyright © 1967 by Elsevier Science, Ltd. Reprinted with the permission of the publishers.

63 H. Jackson Brown, Jr., 60, 175, 212, 217, 251, 286, 318, 435, 448, 450 from *Life's Little Instruction Book: 511 Suggestions, Observations, and Reminders on How to Live a Happy and Rewarding Life*. Copyright © 1991 by H. Jackson Brown, Jr. Reprinted with the permission of Rutledge Hill Press.

77, 82 Paul Wilson, excerpts from *The Little Book of Calm*. Copyright © 1996 by Paul Wilson. Reprinted with the permission of Penguin Putnam Inc.

Illustrations

Ray Alma	8, 27, 43, 51, 57, 69
Carlos Castellanos	9, 31, 65
Bruce Day	56, 75
Andrea Champlin	5, 6, 7 *(top)*, 13, 17, 22, 39, 74, 76, 77, 80 *(top)*, 82, 83, 84 *(bottom)*
Patrick Merrell	32, 41, 49, 62
Andy Myer	3, 16, 80 *(bottom)*
William Waitzman	38, 61, 66, 78, 84 *(top)*, 91

Photographic Credits

The author and publisher are grateful for the permission to reproduce the following photographs:

Cover Photos: background: Darrell Gulin/Corbis; *from top to bottom:* Bruce Ayres/Stone; Jose Luis Pelaez/Corbis/Stock Market; Telegraph Color Library/FPG; Piecework Productions/The Image Bank; Michael Keller/ Pictor; M.J. Cardenas/The Image Bank

2 *(left to right, top to bottom)* Sotographs/Liaison Agency; Tom McCarthy/PhotoEdit; Charles Gupton/Stone; Robert Frerck/Woodfin Camp

8 *(left to right)* Bob Daemmrich/Stock Boston; Bob Daemmrich/The Image Works; Owen Frankin/Corbis

10 *(left to right, top to bottom)* Pictor International/PictureQuest; Reuters/Bob Padgett/Archive Photos; Reuters/Paulo Whitaker/Archive Photos; Photo Van Gasse/Photo News/Liaison Agency; Raphael Gaillarde/Liaison Agency; Jeff Lepore/Photo Researchers

12 20th Century Fox/Everett Collection

14 M.C. Escher's "Relativity" (c) 2000 Cordon Art B.V., Baarn, Holland. All Rights Reserved.

15 *(top left)* Phil Schermeister/Corbis; *(bottom)* Courtesy of Nigel Rogers/Incredible Optical Illusions

20 *(left to right)* Charles Gupton/Stock Boston; Bob Daemmrich/Stock Boston; A. Ramey/Woodfin Camp

24 *(top to bottom)* Neal Peters Collection; Lawrence Schwartzwald/Liaison Agency

26 *(left to right)* Ian Jones/FSP/Liaison Agency; American Stock/Archive Photos; Mark Lennihan/AP/Wide World Photos; Reuters/Jeff Christensen/Archive Photos

28 *(left to right)* Jeff Greenberg/PhotoEdit; Jeff Greenberg/PhotoEdit; Bob Handelman/Stone

34 *(left to right, top to bottom)* Don Mason/Corbis/Stock Market; Mark Richards/PhotoEdit; Philip & Karen Smith/Stone; Reuters/Fabrizio Bensch/Archive Photos; Tony Freeman/PhotoEdit; Alon Reininger/Contact Press

38 *(left to right)* Lara Jo Regan/Liaison Agency; Norbert Wu/Corbis/Stock Market; Don Mason/Corbis/Stock Market

40 *(left to right)* Robert Brenner/PhotoEdit; VCG/FPG; Michael Newman/PhotoEdit

42 *(left to right, top to bottom)* Ed Collacott/Stone; Peter Beck/Pictor; Luis Liwanag/Liaison Agency; Bill Gillette/Liaison Agency; Sheila Beougher/Liaison Agency; Christine Osborne/Corbis

44 *(top)* G. Brad Lewis/Stone; *(right)* Paul Kenward/Stone; *(bottom)* Benjamin Rondel/Corbis/Stock Market

46 *(left to right)* Albert Ferreira/AP/Wide World Photos; Mark Reinstein/FPG; Anchorage Daily News/Bill Roth/AP/Wide World Photos

47 *(top)* Grant L. Gursky/AP/Wide World Photos; *(right)* Reuters/Lee Jae-won/Archive Photos; *(bottom)* Reuters/Chen Ming-hui/Archive Photos

50 *(left to right)* Ron Chapple/FPG; David Young-Wolff/PhotoEdit; Gary Conner/PhotoEdit

58 *(left to right)* Theo Allofs/Stone; Johnny Johnson/DRK Photo; Bilderberg/Corbis/Stock Market

59 *(left to right)* Bill Miles/Corbis/Stock Market; Rob Lewine/Corbis/Stock Market; David Young-Wolff/PhotoEdit

60 *(left to right)* Charles Gupton/Corbis/Stock Market; Chuck Savage/Corbis/Stock Market; S. Rubin/The Image Works

64 *(left)* Josef Polleross/Corbis/Stock Market; *(top)* Barbara Leslie/FPG; *(bottom)* Ariel Skelly/Corbis/Stock Market; *(right)* Yuen Lee/Liaison Agency

67 *(top to bottom)* Jon Eisberg/FPG; Travelpix/FPG

68 *(left to right, top to bottom)* Andrew Yates/The Image Bank; Michael Keller/Pictor; Myrleen Ferguson/PhotoEdit; Lee Snider/The Image Works

71 *(left to right)* Fritz Hoffmann/The Image Works; Windsor Pub/FPG; David R. Frazier; Earl Young/Archive

77 *El Camion*, 1929, by Frida Kahlo/Art Resource/Fundacion Delores Olmedo, Mexico City, D.F., Mexico

80 *The Sleeping Gypsy*, 1897; Henri Rousseau/The Museum of Modern Art, New York. Gift of Simon Guggenheim. Photograph © 2000 The Museum of Modern Art, New York

Every effort has been made to trace the owners of copyright material in this book. We would be grateful to hear from anyone who recognizes their copyright material and who is unacknowledged. We will be pleased to make the neccessary corrections in future editions of the book.